What oth
30 Days to

"Deborah Pegues pulls no .... as she challenges readers to 'get real and deal' with the underlying emotions that fuel their anger. The practical truths in this book will set you free."

Stephen Arterburn, founder and chairman of New Life Ministries,
best-selling author, and host of *New Life Live!*
nationally syndicated radio program

"30 Days to Taming Your Anger presents clear-cut strategies on how to triumph over your mild and major feelings of displeasure while preserving your peace of mind—and your relationships. Read it and grow!"

Marilyn Hickey and Sarah Bowling, hosts of
Today with Marilyn and Sarah international TV program

"Once again, Deborah Pegues forces us to take an objective, biblically based look at ourselves and how we respond to life's issues. From guidelines on how to temper our righteous indignation to controlling nonrelational factors that often lead to anger, this book is chock-full of wisdom that can guarantee your peace of mind. It is a must-read that you will surely refer to often. I know I will!"

Judge Mablean Ephriam, former judge on *Divorce Court*,
author, and speaker on relationship issues

30 DAYS TO
Taming
YOUR
Anger

Deborah Smith Pegues

HARVEST HOUSE PUBLISHERS
EUGENE, OREGON

Cover design by Koechel Peterson & Associates, Inc., Minneapolis, Minnesota

All cover photos © Thinkstock

30 DAYS TO TAMING YOUR ANGER
Copyright © 2013 by Deborah Smith Pegues
Published by Harvest House Publishers
Eugene, Oregon 97402
www.harvesthousepublishers.com

ISBN 978-0-7369-4574-5 (pbk.)
ISBN 978-0-7369-4576-9 (eBook)

Printed in the United States of America

13 14 15 16 17 18 19 20 21 22 / BP-CD / 10 9 8 7 6 5 4 3 2

This book is dedicated to my mother,
Doris Lavon Smith,
who transitioned to her heavenly home on
May 23, 2012.
Her unconditional love, support, and faith in the power of God
inspired me to reach for the stars.

Acknowledgments

I am eternally grateful to the Holy Spirit who carried me during the writing of this book as I faced many challenging circumstances that threatened my focus—including the death of my beloved mother. To Him be all the glory.

My husband, Darnell, is a gift to me in every way. I could never render enough service to God to compensate for His blessing me with such an asset.

My prayer intercessors have been invaluable. Thank you, Pastor Edward Smith, Renee Hernandez, Billie Rodgers, Cheryl Martin, Michelle McKinney Hammond, Diane Gardner, Yvonne Johnson, Terri McFaddin Solomon, Zoe Christian Fellowship of Whittier Life Group leader Jeanette Stone and the awesome ladies, and all who bombarded heaven on my behalf. I love you all.

My "resource" team was awesome with their stories, books, personal experiences, insights, and support. Thank you, Albert Thomas, Pamela Johnson, Elvin Ezekiel, Gerald Johnson, Kari Herreman, Alvin and Pamela Kelley, Kelvin and Delisa Kelley, Ricky and Diane Temple, and the many anonymous contributors. The names in the stories that appear in various chapters have been changed to protect the identities of the individuals.

Thanks to my Harvest House Publishers team: President Bob Hawkins Jr., acquisitions editor Terry Glaspey, senior editor Rod Morris, and the rest of the "dream team" for bringing this project to fruition. Your commitment to producing quality Christian literature is unsurpassed. I'm honored and humbled to be associated with you and to enjoy your favor and support.

Contents

Part 4: Deal with the Nonemotional Anger Triggers

It's a Mad, Mad World

It was Friday afternoon around 3:00 p.m. when I joined the slowing traffic on the Interstate 10 freeway heading for the Los Angeles garment district. I needed to pick up some special buttons to update an outfit I had planned to wear over the weekend. Of course, I should have made the trip earlier in the day, but I had gotten sidetracked responding to emails. Without the heavy traffic, this little excursion usually took less than an hour round-trip.

Within minutes of getting on the freeway, I looked into my rearview mirror and discovered a huge sports utility vehicle just inches from my bumper. I concluded that the tailgater was trying to intimidate me into going faster. I immediately felt *irritated*. He was violating my highway boundaries. I thought, *I should teach him a lesson and drive even slower. Can't he see it's impossible and unsafe to go any faster in this traffic?*

As I contemplated whether to retaliate or to ignore the bully, traffic came to almost a complete stop. No way was my plan of running into my favorite wholesale fabric store, grabbing the buttons, and getting back home by 4:00 p.m. going to work today. I felt extremely *frustrated* with the snail-like pace.

After what seemed an eternity, traffic finally started to inch along again. I decided it was best to exit the freeway and take the surface streets the rest of the way. As I guided my car toward the exit lane, a car came speeding down the shoulder and barely missed me. It scared the daylights out of me. I was *infuriated*! The driver could have killed me. I fantasized about what it would be like to shoot out the windows in his car with a nonlethal weapon specifically designed to punish reckless drivers. In that moment, I understood why some people succumb to road rage.

From the time Cain killed his brother Abel to the 2011 Arab Spring uprising against oppressive government regimes in the Middle East, anger has been one of the primary motivators of negative human behavior. Notwithstanding, even God can be provoked to anger. In fact, there are more references in the Bible to God's anger than to man's. However, God's anger was always in response to man's violation of His covenants or commands.

I am well acquainted with this powerful emotion of anger. I grew up in a household where angry displays occurred as frequently as trips to the market. My dad was a good provider who exercised great financial discipline, but he had a volatile temper. With seven children in the home—including six rambunctious boys and a wife who never quite embraced the idea of a household budget—there was no shortage of behaviors to set him off. Domestic abuse and corporal punishment were the norm. Even when everyone behaved, Dad still always seemed to be angry. At his core, he loved God. He was a faithful deacon, Sunday school superintendent, and a trustworthy church treasurer; nevertheless, his anger would get the best of him. And, like most parents, he passed his legacy of mismanaged anger along to his children.

I used to think that I escaped unscathed as everyone viewed me as the levelheaded one in the family. I refused to succumb to angry outbursts or violence. To this day I cannot recall ever having engaged in a loud argument or having a physical altercation with anyone in my entire life! However, through good mentoring, prayer, studying the Bible, and much self-examination, I learned that I too was mismanaging my anger. I often expressed it by calmly delivering syrupy sarcasm designed to demean my opponent, by cutting offenders out of my life completely, and by finding refuge in food.

We are all so diverse in our perceptions of and responses to anger-triggering events. Most of us struggle with navigating that great chasm between the apostle Paul's two-part admonition, "Be angry" and "do not sin" (Ephesians 4:26). It's time to take control of this powerful emotion and stop letting it control us.

Be forewarned, this book is unapologetically biblical in its approach to dealing with this complex emotion. I say "complex" because even as I ponder my previously mentioned freeway experience, I realize that within moments, I had experienced three degrees of anger:

irritation, frustration, and *infuriation.* Each of these feelings of displeasure has a different depth and duration. My desire is to show you practical ways to minimize and triumph over these emotions. Of course, no discussion of anger would be complete without addressing *indignation*, the good, righteous anger against injustice—anger with a cause. Anger that can often get out of control if our zeal is not restrained.

Since most of the triggers that provoke us to anger are initiated by others, the majority of the book will address such behavior. I will help you to identify your triggers and explore ways to deal with the underlying "pre-anger" or primary emotions that are often at the root of our displeasure.

Finally, I will explain how to triumph over certain external contributors to this *God-given* emotion of protest. Yes, anger is a protest against a real or perceived violation of our principles, our peace, our possessions, our preferences, our plans, our physical well-being, or our personal relationships.

Part 1

Understand the Nature
of the Beast

Irritation: Master Your Triggers

*Irritation: a temporary annoyance
that rouses mild displeasure*

I try to answer my office phone personally whenever possible. It is my attempt to counter the influence of impersonal communication that is the norm today. It irritates me, however, when callers, having learned that they've reached me instead of my assistant, proceed to tell me their entire life story in long-drawn-out details. Even after I pray with them and encourage them, I fight the temptation to become irritated.

Irritation is the mildest form of anger and has the shortest duration. Irritation is inescapable in everyday life. I'm sure you could produce a list of behaviors that regularly irritate or annoy you. Perhaps you can relate to some common triggers others have expressed:

"Inconsiderate mobile phone users"

"Rude or uncaring customer service"

"Drivers who ride your bumper"

"People who move too slowly"

"Folks who violate my personal space"

"Parents who ignore their children's annoying behavior in public"

"People who drop by without calling first"

"An invited guest who brings an *uninvited* guest to my sit-down dinner party"

"People who engage in 'sidebar' conversations while someone else has the floor"

"Shoppers with twenty items who get in the ten-items-or-less line—in front of me"

"People who address me as 'honey,' 'sweetheart,' or any other term of endearment"

"Street beggars who are mean or ungrateful"

These short-term displeasures not only provoke our impatience but can also threaten our peace if we let them. If you live on Planet Earth, where people don't always behave as they should, you would do well to develop some good coping strategies. Otherwise, mismanaged irritations can quickly turn into full-blown anger with destructive consequences.

Although some behaviors can be confronted in an assertive, God-honoring way (like the time a fellow college student looked at me imploringly and stated that my gum chewing was driving her crazy), many irritations leave us with few options beyond accepting or ignoring them. King Solomon admonished, "A person's wisdom yields patience; it is to one's glory to overlook an offense" (Proverbs 19:11 NIV). And, yes, I know it takes special grace to overlook things that get under our skin—but the secret is to embrace the grace God gives for every situation.

Grace is God's empowering ability to do through us what we cannot do in our own strength. Every Spirit-filled person bears the seeds of love, peace, joy, and long-suffering—the fruit of the Spirit (Galatians 5:22-23) that give us the victory over irritations. The problem is that like natural fruit, the fruit of the Spirit must be *developed*; they do not naturally or automatically manifest as our first response to the challenges of life. They take practice, practice, practice. Once we commit to intentionally exercising them, we will consistently advance to higher levels of spiritual and emotional maturity.

Another key to maintaining our peace when we encounter an irritation-triggering event is to change our perspective. Most of us tend to evaluate other people's actions through our personal lens. We focus on how *we* would behave in the situation:

"*I'm* always mindful of my volume when using my mobile phone in public."

"*I* keep a proper physical distance when interacting with others, never violating their space."

"*I* would never do that."

"*I…*," "*I…*," "*I…*"

What we don't realize is that this mindset sets us up as judge and jury in the case of those who do not conduct themselves as they "should." I'm convinced that if we limited or even eliminated the word *should* from our thoughts and our expressions, we would experience less inner turmoil.

I should know. I grew up in a strict Pentecostal environment where shoulds, rules, and legalistic expectations reigned. Later in life, I found myself constantly irritated with people who didn't do what I thought they should—spiritually, financially, relationally, or socially. It goes without saying that I was always in a mode of judging others.

If you find yourself caught in a "should trap," here are three surefire escape hatches:

1. When you feel that someone's irritating behavior will become a pattern if you do not address it, calmly explain to the person how her actions affect you and ask her to stop. *Example 1:* "Karen, when I invite you to dinner, the invitation is extended to you only. Please do not ask someone else to join you without consulting me first." *Example 2:* "Would you mind holding down your voices? I'm having a hard time hearing the speaker." (No need to call them rude or inconsiderate.)

2. Rather than judging or criticizing the offensive behavior, engage in a little self-interrogation instead:

   • What personal preference or strongly held belief/tradition is this person violating?

   • Is any real harm being done here to me or to others?

   • Does the offender remind me of another irritating person I need to confront?

- Is the offender mirroring an aspect of my own behavior that I disdain?

- What response to this irritation would be the most honoring to my heavenly Father?

3. Give the offender the benefit of the doubt or seek to understand his shortcomings. For example, the tailgater may not be intent on bullying you but simply has poor driving habits. The inconsiderate mobile phone user is not deliberately annoying you but is merely too self-focused to think about how he's affecting others. The boss who takes all the credit for the success of the project is simply an insecure leader with poor management skills.

Choosing the responses above is where the fruit of love comes into play; for "love will cover a multitude of sins" (1 Peter 4:8). Further, do you really want to let temporary, non-eternal matters rob you of your peace and joy?

Faith Declaration

The Holy Spirit is manifesting the fruit of love, joy, and peace in me right now and empowering me to respond with patience to every irritation.

Day 2

Frustration: Know When to Hold 'em or Fold 'em

*Frustration: a feeling of displeasure toward
an obstacle (person, event, or physical
barrier) that hinders your progress toward
a goal or fails to meet your expectation*

Life hasn't been easy for Carrie. Born out of wedlock, she saw her father on only a few occasions during her entire childhood. She was raised primarily by her godly and strict grandmother while her own mother worked to help support them all. During her last year in high school, Carrie became pregnant by a young man who chose to have nothing to do with their daughter, Sadie. Undaunted, Carrie and her mother tried to give Sadie all the comforts of life. However, living such a privileged existence didn't give Sadie much incentive to survive on her own. After high school, Sadie never quite got her act together. To this day she continues to be plagued with relational and financial drama.

In addition to dealing with Sadie's woes, Carrie's aging mother requires increasingly more time and attention. Further, her husband, Jim, could find work only out of state, so he relocated fifteen hundred miles away and could afford to come home only twice a year. This lasted for over a decade! In the midst of it all, Carrie developed an advanced stage of breast cancer. After extended chemotherapy, surgery, and an outpouring of prayers, she won the battle and is now cancer free. However, she was forced to close down her small restaurant— a business she had built from scratch.

Then came the 2008 economic downturn. Jim was laid off from his job. Even though his skills were now relatively marketable in their hometown, he opted for early retirement. He returned home content to live on his meager pension rather than seek contract work, much to Carrie's dismay. Further, because Carrie is known for her survivor skills and positive mindset, she is the go-to counselor and sounding board for the majority of her relatives and friends.

Despite experiencing one frustrating situation after another, Carrie maintains a tremendous sense of humor, a no-nonsense communication style, clear boundaries in her relationships, and a commitment to her mental and physical well-being. She's quick to acknowledge circumstances that are outside of her control. She often exclaims, "I'm not going to let these folks and their issues kill me!" She finds refuge in fishing, engaging in home-decorating projects, and serving her community. When the pressures of life mount, she has been known to hop in her car and drive across the country alone to get away from it all. Carrie knows how to master frustration.

What about you? Are you frustrated for one reason

or another with your spouse, boss, child, or others in your circle of interaction? Maybe you are even frustrated with God! Have your frustrations affected your emotional well-being or brought you to the brink of an angry reaction?

I fought being frustrated with God when He called me off my dream job in 2006 to speak and write full-time—only to find myself six months later battling a neurological condition (trigeminal neuralgia) that frequently rendered me speechless with no advance warning. I stood in faith for my healing. However, there were times that I wondered, "What gives? I'm just trying to obey You. I could have stayed on my job where I had sick leave and other benefits!"

As an act of faith, I continued to schedule speaking engagements and media interviews. I often showed up not knowing if I'd be able to talk or not. At one conference, I had to place a wad of small makeup sponges inside my jaw to minimize the excruciating pain caused by the movement of my mouth; the protruding jaw was a curious sight.

I refused to get depressed. I believed then as I do today that "the joy of the Lord is [my] strength" (Nehemiah 8:10) and that all things work together for my good because I love God and I'm called according to His purpose (Romans 8:28). After fourteen months of debilitating pain, I underwent brain surgery. By the grace of God, I experienced no side effects. I developed inner strength, a greater sense of dependence on Him, and a new level of faith.

Frustrating people or circumstances are inevitable, but you can master your response to them. Here's how:

- Face the reality of which situations are *controllable* (problems with your boss, pastor, spouse, child, or friend; violations of your boundaries or preferences) and which are *noncontrollable* (changing someone's affections toward you or others).

- In controllable situations, exercise courage by taking the necessary actions to address or eliminate the frustration (confront the offender in a loving manner, seek another job, set relationship boundaries with appropriate consequences, exit toxic relationships). Don't delay. Procrastination here will only solidify your frustration.

- Reevaluate your expectations. Consider if you are being inflexible or unreasonable. Maybe you have too many shoulds for yourself or others. This is a prime area for blind spots, so get some objective input from a wise outsider here.

- For the noncontrollable issues, recognize your limitation and stop attempting to do what only God can do—"know when to hold 'em, know when to fold 'em." (These lyrics to a popular song by Kenny Rogers refer to a gambler's decision to stay in or get out of the game depending on the hand he has been dealt. We use the phrase in various personal or business situations to describe the decision to pursue an effort or to throw in the towel.) When you come to grips with the reality that you cannot influence a certain frustrating situation, halt your efforts and limit your involvement to praying for divine intervention.

• Hide Scriptures in your heart that emphasize the perfect wisdom and timing of God for your life. For starters see the "Faith Declaration" below. Accept His plan and His schedule—not with sad resignation but with an attitude of gratitude for His foreknowledge of all that concerns you and His desire for the best outcome.

Faith Declaration

"All the days ordained for me were written in [God's] book before one of them came to be" (Psalm 139:16 NIV), therefore, no one can thwart His plan for my life (Isaiah 14:27). I will exercise the courage to do what my Father would have me to do to overcome controllable frustrations and the wisdom to entrust the noncontrollable situations entirely to Him. The Holy Spirit is working the fruit of patience in my heart right now. I accept God's will to be done His way in every aspect of my life.

Day 3

Infuriation: Deactivate Your Buttons

Infuriate: *to enrage; to provoke
to wrath or revenge*

Our pastor had called the congregation to a twenty-one-day Daniel Fast during which we abstained from meats, sweets, and our favorite treats. It was Day 21—the last day—and I was glad God had given me the grace to complete it thus far. Darnell and I entered the Soup and Salad buffet restaurant totally famished. While he paid the bill, I found a strategically located booth, put my tray down, and headed for the salad and soup bar. I was already imagining what joy I would experience as I combined several different soups in one bowl (sounds yucky, but it's delicious).

When I returned to the table, another couple was sitting there and the tray was gone! I was infuriated by this apparent violation of our right to that table. My vision blurred with rage, probably more from the hunger than the perceived injustice (at this point the two were impossible to differentiate). However, having taught effective confrontation for over twenty years, I thought I'd better practice what I preach. About this time, the waiter assigned to that section appeared on the scene.

"What happened here?" I calmly asked. "I had placed my tray at this table."

"Oh, I am so sorry," she said. "I took it away. I didn't know the table was occupied."

The couple looked perplexed and offered to move. I started to accept their offer but considered this might be a good time to give the fruit of the Spirit an opportunity to prevail—after all, we were on a fast for *spiritual* growth. I decided to extend mercy to the server and simply find another table.

As I reflected on the incident later, I was disappointed that I had allowed myself to become furious over an insignificant act. When I considered the global issue of world hunger, why would I be so upset about losing the "ideal" table for my feast when billions of people have no food to put on a table? I felt ashamed and unspiritual.

My first step in understanding my anger was to identify the root cause. I started my self-interrogation. *What button was pushed here?* The answer came in seconds: I detest incompetence. With my tendency to be performance oriented, it's no surprise that my motto is, "If you are going to do a job, do it well!" What I had immediately judged as incompetence was simply human error. Once again I needed to remind myself that we are human *beings*, not human *doings*. I thought, *Deborah, it's time to deactivate that incompetence button. Get out of the mode of always evaluating people's performance!*

What about you? What are some things that people do that enrage you and cause you to feel a level of anger beyond irritation or frustration? I'm talking about behaviors that make you want to retaliate, to exact revenge, or to mete out some form of punishment. I hope this is a very short or nonexistent list. However, there's a good chance this could be a problem area since you're reading this book. This is an important self-discovery exercise. Once you are aware of what infuriates you, you can identify the triggering event and keep people or situations from getting the best of you.

The key to preventing rage is to prepare in advance (where possible), especially if you have to interact frequently with someone who pushes your rage buttons. Most people who habitually push your buttons know from your response that there is power in their actions, power to make you feel diminished, frustrated, or discontent. Your challenge is to respond in such a way that they know you have disconnected their power cord and are "dead" to their provocation. This means that you must commit to maintaining a calm and peaceful attitude. *Peacefulness is the place of power.* Don't relinquish your power to the button pusher. Say to yourself as you breathe slowly and deeply, *If I stay peaceful, I'll stay powerful. The Holy Spirit is flooding my mind with peace right now.*

The next step to avoid becoming infuriated in interpersonal interactions is to consider the source. For example, if someone teases you about your weight gain or that you are much older than she, or brags on someone (in your field) who is more successful, it is highly likely the person feels inferior to you in some way and is trying to level the playing field. Consider the source and develop a lighthearted response that is not dishonoring to God. Sure, you could deliver a cutting comeback, but there is no power or growth in that. Rather, try a response such as:

"What a blessing to get older; I'm enjoying the wisdom that comes with aging."

"Losing weight is a real challenge when you are blessed with such abundance. What's your secret?"

But, you may ask, "What about the rage aroused by strangers? How do I respond if someone crashes into my car?" Relax. You're human. It's natural to feel extreme displeasure when you are suddenly disadvantaged. But the deed is done; you can't undo it. Ask yourself, *What course of action do I take next?* Thoughts of revenge or a verbal attack will serve no purpose. Be smart here.

Just last weekend I became incensed at our neighbor (a really nice person), who has eight cars on our congested cul-de-sac of only ten houses. He parked one of his cars in front of our house, taking the only parking space we have for guests. I felt disadvantaged. However, my husband reminded me that homeowners do not own the street in front of their house. Besides, we weren't expecting guests. Was it really worth making it an issue with the neighbor when he had willingly cooperated in the past when we were expecting guests?

You have to be intentional in managing your rage and know when you are progressing to that stage in your emotions. In subsequent chapters we will explore specific ways to deal with rage as well as the underlying emotions that give rise to such intense feelings.

Faith Declaration

When I am tempted to give in to rage, I will say to myself,
"Stop being angry!
Turn from your rage!
Do not lose your temper—
it only leads to harm."
(Psalm 37:8 NLT)

Day 4

Indignation: Be Good and Angry

Indignation: *strong displeasure over something considered unjust, offensive, insulting, or wrong; righteous anger*

On July 29, 1994, Dr. John Britton and his bodyguard, James Barrett, were shot to death outside a Pensacola abortion clinic. Rev. Paul Jennings Hill was charged with the killings. He told reporters that he believed he would get a reward in heaven. He received a death sentence. At his execution in September 2003, the unremorseful defrocked minister gave these final words, "The last thing I want to say: If you believe abortion is a lethal force, you should oppose the force and do what you have to do to stop it. May God help you to protect the unborn as you would want to be protected."[1]

Hill was just one of many whose indignation over the killing of unborn babies has driven them to engage in vandalism, bombings, murder, and other acts of violence against people or places connected with providing abortions.

Indignation is the God-given emotion of anger that

can serve anger's best purpose—seeking to right a wrong or to solve a problem. We have every right (at least in the United States) to protest inequities and to seek ways to redress wrongs, but we do not have a right to break laws. Henry Ward Beecher, American clergyman and social reformer, declared, "A person that does not know how to be angry does not know how to be good." Mahatma Gandhi and Rev. Martin Luther King Jr. were "indignants," but they were committed to nonviolence in their protests.

Christians who engage in unlawful acts to right a wrong often justify their misbehavior. They misinterpret Scripture such as Proverbs 31:9 (NLT): "Yes, speak up for the poor and helpless, and see that they get justice." They fail to recognize that the core message here is to speak up—not to beat up or tear up. Supreme Court Justice Oliver Wendell Holmes Jr. declared, "The right to swing my fist ends where the other man's nose begins."

Of course, we cannot claim that the love of God dwells in us if we can stand by, say nothing, and do nothing while innocent, helpless people are mistreated or exploited. However, harming others is not an option that *individuals* should consider. (I am in no way condemning a *country's* right to protect its citizens through whatever means necessary.)

To manage this God-approved anger, you must first get to the core of your personal motivation for it. Rather than springing from a heart of love for God and humankind, your indignation could be arising from your adherence to man-made traditions, your private interpretation of Scripture, or your prejudices.

For instance, I grew up in a strict Southern culture where almost *everything* was a sin except eating. When I relocated to Los Angeles, I was frequently offended and filled with indignation at the behavior of West Coast Christians—from men and women swimming in the same pool to women wearing sleeveless dresses to church (no kidding!). Finally, I just asked God to show me His standard of behavior for me, to take away my judgmental attitude, and to help me to be offended only by sin and injustice. I haven't arrived in this area, but I have certainly left the station.

Righteous indignation in the Bible always involved a defense of others or the protection of a moral principle. Nathan the prophet related a story to King David about a rich man who took a poor man's prized and only lamb and slaughtered it rather than one from his own flock for his guest. David immediately became incensed and declared that the selfish rich man must die. Of course the story was a setup to help David see that his adultery with Bathsheba and the killing of her husband to hide his sin were tantamount to the actions of the rich man (2 Samuel 12). Notwithstanding, David's heart response was to defend the disadvantaged.

Most Bible readers are also familiar with the account of Jesus overthrowing the tables of the moneychangers and chasing them out of the temple because they were defiling it with their commercial activity. No way was he going to allow God's house to become a den of thieves (John 2:13-18).

This is the type of anger that God exhibits. It is a holy

anger aroused by violation of His laws and principles. He has the wisdom to be angry but to remain good.

> Who can stand before His indignation?
> And who can endure the fierceness of His
>   anger?…
> The LORD is good,
> A stronghold in the day of trouble;
> And He knows those who trust in Him.
>
> (Nahum 1:6,7)

We must continue to be indignant about injustices. We must make every effort to make a difference in an often-indifferent world. We can sign petitions, participate in email campaigns, march for the disadvantaged, vote and pray the bums out of political office, and engage in other constructive acts of protest. But for goodness' sake, let's remind ourselves of the moral theory that one man's rights end where another's begin. Most of all, let's remember the psalmist's admonition: "Be angry, and do not sin" (Psalm 4:4).

Faith Declaration

Motivated by a heart of love for God and my fellow-man, I will control my indignation and vigorously defend moral principles and justice for others with wisdom and respect for the rights of the transgressors.

Part 2

Evaluate Your Response Options

Day 5

Pull Off the Passive Path

To everything there is a season, a time
for every purpose under heaven...
A time to keep silence, and a time to speak.
ECCLESIASTES 3:1,7

Meet Passive Pat. She makes every effort to accommodate requests from others no matter how much inconvenience, time, or money it costs. Many take her kindness for granted and habitually violate her personal boundaries. Nevertheless, she trudges along life's pathway doing what she feels she should as a good single parent, daughter, sister, coworker, church member, or friend.

Why, just last Saturday evening she was getting ready to attend a much-anticipated banquet when her recently divorced son dropped off his twin boys, promising to "be back in a flash." Three hours later, Pat gave up trying to reach him on his cell phone. Around midnight, he showed up with a sheepish grin on his face and exclaimed, "I think I just met my next wife!" Pat was livid but remained calm; inside, her emotions raged like *The Towering Inferno*.

People who choose such a passive response to their anger usually hold certain erroneous beliefs that may include one or more of the following:

- "Being angry is sinful." (Ephesians 4:26 allows us to experience anger but to avoid a sinful response.)

- "It's unladylike to show anger." (That's just ancient thinking!)

- "If I rock the boat, I'll ruin the relationship." (Press past your fear of rejection; you bring something of value to the table too.)

- "If I get angry, I might lose complete control and regret it later." (Not if you confront the issue timely and calmly.)

Trapped by these beliefs, the Passive Pats of the world respond to anger-inducing situations in various ways: becoming silent, conveniently forgetting to perform a task, gossiping or spreading nasty rumors about the offender, being sarcastic, damaging the offender's property, withholding sex from an offending spouse, withholding critical information, seeking comfort from food, alcohol, or drugs, undereating, or withdrawing from the environment, to name a few.

It was this last option that the prodigal son's brother (whom we will call Sibling 1) chose in expressing his anger (see Luke 15:11-32). His younger brother had requested advance payment of his inheritance, moved away, and squandered it all on fast living. He returned home repentant and broke. His father, rather than rejecting him or finding a way to teach him a lesson, received him with open arms. Further, the father unknowingly added insult to injury (at least from Sibling 1's perspective), by throwing the prodigal a big party. No way was Sibling 1 going to celebrate such irresponsibility:

> "The older brother was angry and wouldn't go in. His father came out and begged him, but he replied, 'All these years I've slaved for you and never once refused to do a single thing you told me to. And in all that time you never gave me even one young goat for a feast with my friends. Yet when this son of yours comes back after squandering your money on prostitutes, you celebrate by killing the fattened calf!'" (Luke 15:28-30 NLT).

I applaud Sibling 1 for finally expressing that he felt taken for granted. (Of course his lack of compassion for a repentant soul is another issue and not to be applauded.) Nevertheless, it is important to express how you feel when conflicts or offenses occur. This is hard for most people as it is learned behavior and most of our parents didn't model or teach it.

In my book *Confronting Without Offending*, I give specific guidelines for confronting people when their behavior has negatively affected you. Our primary challenge is simply to say, "I am hurt or offended by your actions." How will people ever know if you don't tell them? Otherwise, they are likely to repeat the behavior.

Try these steps and strategies if you want to get on the path to overcoming passive expressions of your anger:

- Recall the most recent incident in which your anger was aroused and you chose not to address it with the offender.

- Acknowledge the erroneous belief(s), such as those listed above, that caused you to send your feelings "underground."

- Name one benefit or value you add to your relationship with the offender (support, loyalty, and so on). How important do you think this is to her? This step helps you to understand that you bring something worthwhile to the table. Do not conclude that you hold an inferior position in any relationship simply because you have less money, education, worldly beauty, or whatever.

- Stand in front of a mirror and practice making the assertive, God-honoring statement you *wish* you had expressed at the time of the incident. Even though it is after the fact, you're developing the skill of choosing the right words to say in a future situation.

- Consider what you could have said or what boundaries you could have established prior to the incident that may have prevented its occurrence.

- If you have decided that it's much too scary to confront hurtful or offensive behavior and that it is safer to stay on the passive path, reflect on the consequences of holding in your anger. Potential ailments that mental health professionals generally agree are sometimes associated with passive anger include: asthma, jaw problems from grinding one's teeth, skin problems (rashes, eczema, boils, pimples), ulcers, obesity, alcoholism, bad breath, bursitis, carpal tunnel, earaches, kidney stones, thyroid problems, sexual problems, liver problems, rheumatoid arthritis, chronic fatigue, chronic sore throats, and urinary infections. More serious conditions include strokes, diabetes, and heart attacks. The emotional toll includes decreased self-esteem and increased self-loathing. Now, is it really worth keeping quiet and burying your anger alive?

Faith Declaration

When someone sins against me, I will do as Jesus commanded: I will go and tell him his fault privately (Matthew 18:15). I will be calm, honest, and open to a mutually agreeable solution to the problem.

Abandon Aggressive Actions

*Let all bitterness, wrath, anger,
clamor, and evil speaking be put
away from you, with all malice.*

Ephesians 4:31

Supermodel Naomi Campbell is almost as famous for her out-of-control temper as she is for her work in the fashion industry. News reports have highlighted her aggressive behavior, which has included throwing a phone at her maid, attacking two policemen at London's Heathrow airport, whacking her limo driver on the back of the head, and hitting a cameraman when she stormed out of a television interview, to name a few.

Displeasure expressed in this way is *aggression*. It is intended to hurt the other person physically or emotionally. Put-downs, yelling, threatening, and exhibiting any form of violence are examples of aggression.

In the previous chapter, we saw the pitfalls of passivity. As we consider this second option for responding to anger-provoking people or situations, let's first take a quick personal inventory.

- Do you express your point of view with an

arrogant attitude that implies it's the last word regarding the matter?

- Are you so focused on your own needs that you deem everybody else's unimportant?

- Do you often pretend to be outraged because it makes you feel powerful to see others cower in the face of your intimidation?

- After an outburst, do you feel remorseful or guilty when your victim withdraws from you?

If you answered yes to any of the above questions, I'm going to assume that you are serving a sentence in the prison of aggression. Here's how to be set free:

- Take control of your physical symptoms by breathing deeply so that you stay rational in your thinking. The George Washington University Counseling Center gives this advice:

  When you feel angry, it is important to have a relaxation technique that works quickly and in any situation. Deep breathing allows the body to absorb more oxygen and slows your heart rate to combat the adrenaline rush that floods the body when you're angry. Deep breathing involves breathing from your stomach area or diaphragm, rather than breathing from your chest and shoulders. When you are engaged in deep breathing, your stomach should move in and out but your chest and shoulders should not move. Deep breathing is rhythmic and slow, similar to your breathing pattern when you sleep.

When you feel yourself becoming angry, take a moment to notice your breathing. Often it will be shallow and quick. If you begin to breathe from your diaphragm and breathe more slowly, you should notice a change in your body. Your muscles may start to relax and the feeling of tension may diminish. This brief pause may also give you a chance to regain your composure, control your angry feelings, change your thoughts, and handle the situation more effectively.[2]

- Expose and disarm your trigger. Rage is unique to each individual based on his history of pain or abuse at the hands of another. Therefore, you must be very honest and deeply introspective as you answer the question, "Why does this enrage me?" You may want to identify your primary underlying feeling by reviewing the list of primary emotions in Part 3.

- Refuse to "live by the sword." When threatened with the loss of someone or something that we value, we can become enraged at the perpetrator and resort to acts of aggression. If we don't develop a more effective way of dealing with such threats, we will become the victims of our own aggression. Our "sword" or habitual act of aggression will kill our relationships, our chance for promotions, our freedom (literally, if incarcerated), and other benefits we were destined to enjoy.

- Adopt a divine perspective on the triggering event. Jesus understood something that Peter did not. "Don't you realize that I could ask my Father for thousands of angels to protect us, and he would send them instantly? But if I did, how would the Scriptures be fulfilled that describe what *must happen* now?" (Matthew 26:53-54 NLT). Jesus maintained His sense of destiny throughout the entire ordeal of the Crucifixion. He understood that some adversities "must happen" to bring us into God's purpose. Contrary to much popular teaching, we are not immune to suffering. If we respond in an aggressive way to perceived injuries or injustices, we may very well thwart their purpose. Further, if we "live by the sword," planting seeds of violence and other forms of harshness in our dealings with others, we are bound to reap a harvest of aggression.

- Practice assertive communication. Learning to express your anger in a calm and direct manner will make you much more effective and powerful while still honoring God. I'll show you how to do it in the next chapter.

Faith Declaration

I am "swift to hear, slow to speak, slow to wrath" (James 1:19). By the grace of God, I resist all acts of aggression. Instead, I allow Him to use every experience to hone me for my destiny.

Day 7

Assert Yourself Appropriately

*"Moreover if your brother sins
against you, go and tell him his fault
between you and him alone…"*
MATTHEW 18:15

The board of directors of X Corporation (a popular charity) was winding down its December meeting. They had just voted unanimously to give Samuel Burns, the general manager of the new building project, a five-figure bonus. Their decision was not based on any performance standards, construction savings, or other objective criteria. Samuel had simply been shrewd enough to negotiate the bonus clause in his employment contract.

Donna, the chief financial officer, was incensed. She marveled that no one on the male-dominated board thought to consider her for a bonus. She had sterling credentials and documented operational savings that she was savvy enough to regularly highlight to the board. Further, she worked an average ten to twelve hours per day in an effort to maintain a lean staff. Her efficiency and value to the organization were undisputed. Samuel, on the other hand, had hired several outside contractors to help with his workload and rarely worked overtime.

Now, Donna was assertiveness personified; she never resorted to passivity or aggression in communicating her displeasure. Rather than fuming, she mentally crafted her response to the disturbing vote and waited for the right time to address it. She breathed deeply, prayed silently, and meditated on her go-to Scripture for such situations: "The Lord GOD has given Me the tongue of the learned, that I should know how to speak a word in season…" (Isaiah 50:4). When she felt the time was right and her emotions were under control, she calmly asked, "Would you like for me to leave the room now while you discuss *my* bonus? In fact, if it's okay, I can finish my financial presentations and leave for the evening."

There was no hostility in her voice. The silence was so thick you could cut it with a knife. After what seemed like an eternity, one of the members said, "Yes, that's a good idea." Donna concluded her final special report and left the meeting. The next day, the CEO informed her that the board had voted to give her a five-figure bonus also. Donna knew that the best way to communicate her expectations was to express them directly and in a nonthreatening way to the person(s) involved. She was also confident of her value to the company.

Acting appropriately assertive is the third option we have in responding to anger. In assertive communication, we state our feelings, expectations, boundaries, desires, or opinions openly but in a tactful and respectful manner. The popular "I" statement model, in which you express to a person in a nonhostile, nonaccusatory manner how his behavior has negatively affected you ("When you ____, I feel____"), is still the best template for an assertive response to anger. Here are some examples:

Husband to wife: "I feel disregarded when you commit us to a social function without consulting me. I'd like you to start clearing such outings with me first."

Employee to supervisor: "When you raise your voice at me—especially in the presence of others—I feel disrespected and demoralized. This really affects my productivity. I'd like you to speak to me privately when you are dissatisfied with my work."

Sibling to sibling: "I feel frustrated when I have to take off from work and drive thirty miles to Mom's house to take her to the doctor, and you live only ten minutes from her. I need you to share this responsibility. Is there a day of the week that's better for you to help out with her needs?"

Notice that in each of these examples, the confronter *described* the problem, *expressed* how he felt about it, and *asked* for a change in behavior. This sounds simple, but it's not always easy—especially for women. We often find ourselves faced with the dilemma of choosing between being liked or respected. Many of us, because we have been socialized to cherish unity, choose to be liked. Further, there is still a tendency in many business and other environments to view assertiveness in a woman as aggression, while an aggressive male is viewed as decisive or no-nonsense. This demonstrates the need for women to develop the skill of mastering their emotions when expressing anger, while at the same time clearly stating their desires.

Whether male or female, to be assertive in expressing anger you must first stop seeing yourself as being inferior or subservient in the relationship. Further, you must believe that you have the God-given right to enjoy your life, to be treated with respect, and to be as individual as you choose to be (without explanation or justification) in the decisions you make for your life. Most importantly, you must believe that others have those same rights.

As you learn to move away from the extreme poles of passivity and aggression, you will find that assertiveness, though it may seem risky, has great rewards:

- You will experience less tension, drama, and stress in your life.

- Your self-respect will be enhanced when you refuse to be a doormat.

- Your productivity and satisfaction at work will increase.

- You will avoid the physical and emotional pitfalls of passive anger.

- You will have healthy and rewarding relationships.

Faith Declaration

The LORD is my light and my salvation;
Whom shall I fear?
The LORD is the strength of my life;
Of whom shall I be afraid?

                         (Psalm 27:1)

Part 3

Master Your Underlying Emotions

Day 8

Afraid

"To be furious, is to be frighted out of fear."
WILLIAM SHAKESPEARE

"Karl, where is Madison?" Stella asked as she set the groceries on the kitchen counter.

"I thought she went to the store with you," Karl said.

They exchanged an anxious look. Karl immediately bounded out the door and down the street in search of his five-year-old granddaughter. He and Stella had won custody of her over a year ago. She was the love of his life. He wouldn't even allow himself to imagine the unthinkable. Madison had several friends who lived on their cul-de-sac, so Karl went from door to door. No one had seen her. He grew more panicky by the moment. Just as he approached the last house, he caught a glimpse of her bicycle in the backyard. He held his breath as he rang the doorbell. Mrs. Johnson opened the door with a warm smile. The aroma of fresh-baked cookies floated from the kitchen.

"Hello. Is Madison over here?" he asked.

"Why, yes she is. She and Sally are having a snack. Madison is such a delight."

Karl felt an overwhelming sense of relief. Then it turned into anger when Madison innocently appeared.

"Madison! What were you thinking?" he yelled. "We had no idea where you were. Let's go—now! When you get home, you're going to get the worst spanking ever!"

He kept his word.

Joseph and Mary had a similar experience with Jesus when he was twelve years old. They took Him to the annual Feast of the Passover in Jerusalem. However, on the return trip home, they discovered that He was not a part of their caravan. They returned to Jerusalem and frantically searched for Him. After three anxious days, they found Him in the temple holding an audience with the Jewish teachers. Although they were impressed with His wisdom, Mary's fear and frustration were obvious.

> So when they saw Him, they were amazed; and His mother said to Him, "Son, why have You done this to us? Look, Your father and I have sought You anxiously."
>
> And He said to them, "Why did you seek Me? Did you not know that I must be about My Father's business?" (Luke 2:48-49).

Fear is underneath most instances of anger. When I was a child, my father was known for giving us a severe spanking whenever we sustained an injury while playing—even before he and my mother rushed us to the hospital. He simply did not know how to deal with the unknown outcome of our getting hurt.

Think about how fear has been at the root of your

anger. For instance, the last time someone almost caused you to have an auto accident, the primary emotion you felt was probably fear of personal injury to yourself or your passengers or damage to your car. I can recall being really upset with a former employee for all the errors I found in a critical report we were preparing for my boss. In analyzing the situation later, I realized that I feared I would have been negatively evaluated based on his performance. After all, I'd hired him.

Now, jealousy—the fear of being displaced—is the most common instance of the relationship between fear and anger. Some people get angry when another person of the opposite sex pays too much attention to their spouse or significant other. Perhaps for most, it would be too painful to admit they fear the loss of affection or even abandonment. They choose rather to allow their insecurity to turn them into an angry person with fractured and unfulfilling relationships.

So, what do you do when you are plagued with fears that cause you to become irritated, frustrated, or even infuriated?

- Be honest about this primary emotion and ask yourself, *What exactly do I fear losing—money, possessions, favor, reputation, a relationship, physical well-being, or other personal ideals?*

- Know that combating one negative emotion (fear) with another (anger) is like fighting fire with fire. Fear does not come from your heavenly Father (2 Timothy 1:7). Therefore, you don't have to tolerate it. Surrender everything you prize or value to Him and trust Him to protect it. "LORD, you alone are my inheritance, my cup of blessing. You guard all that is mine" (Psalm 16:5 NLT).

- Daily declare your freedom from the bondage of fear by praying the Word of God. Below is an excerpt of a prayer from my book *30 Days to Taming Your Fears* that shows you how to do just that:

Father, You are my refuge and my strength, a very present help in my time of trouble. Therefore, I will not fear (Psalm 46:1-2). Thank You in advance for working things out for Your glory and for my good according to Your divine plan and purpose (Romans 8:28). I boldly resist the spirit of fear now and command it to flee (James 4:7). Thank You that Your peace, which surpasses my understanding, is guarding my heart and my mind (Philippians 4:7). Therefore, I will not let my heart be troubled neither will I let it be afraid (John 14:27). In the name of Jesus, I pray. Amen.[3]

Faith Declaration

I constantly seek the Lord and He hears me and delivers me from all my fears (see Psalm 34:4).

Day 9

Disappointed

You can make many plans,
but the LORD's purpose will prevail.
PROVERBS 19:21 NLT

Lisa and her husband, Dean, were the loving parents of three teen daughters. They were a model Christian family that faithfully attended weekly church services. As godly parents, Lisa and Dean held high expectations for their daughters and envisioned an ideal future for them as college grads and happily married wives and mothers. However, their middle daughter, Christy, an honor student, dashed their hopes when she was in her sophomore year of high school. She and her boyfriend, Ted, made the heartbreaking announcement that Christy was pregnant. Lisa was devastated. Dean was in shock.

"How could this happen to our family?" Lisa sobbed to her husband.

"How could God let us down?" Dean said.

They struggled to come to grips with the reality they had been dealt. They were angry with Christy, Ted, and even God for allowing her to conceive.

However, underneath their anger lay the real emotion:

disappointment. After much prayer and soul-searching, Lisa and Dean realized that their disappointment could take them down one of two roads. One led to disgust, anger, and fractured relationships; the other—the one God commands His children to take—led to grace and forgiveness.

In their hearts, they knew that only God could initiate a life; abortion was out of the question. After all, no one knows the destiny God has for every precious life He allows to come into the world. Imagine if the parents of Stanley Ann Dunham, an eighteen-year-old white college freshman, had forced her to abort her child when she found herself pregnant by her African boyfriend. Who knew that she had conceived Barack Obama, the forty-fourth and first African-American president of the United States?

King David understood disappointment. After many frustrating years of running from King Saul, who made numerous attempts on his life, David had finally become king over all of Israel. One of his top priorities was to relocate the ark of the covenant to the capital city. The ark was the most sacred and revered object among the Israelites. It contained the original tablets of stone God gave to Moses at Mount Sinai. It represented the very presence of God Himself. Over thirty thousand choice men accompanied David to celebrate the momentous transport. However, things did not go as planned.

> But when they arrived at the threshing floor of Nacon, the oxen stumbled, and Uzzah reached out his hand and steadied the Ark of God. Then the LORD's anger

was aroused against Uzzah, and God struck him dead because of this. So Uzzah died right there beside the Ark of God.

David was angry because the LORD's anger had burst out against Uzzah (2 Samuel 6:6-8 NLT).

Times of disappointment present the perfect opportunity to reevaluate our goals and expectations, where we place our trust, and how we respond when things do not go our way. Below are five strategies David modeled in his response to the disappointing ark fiasco. You too can do this:

- Acknowledge your disappointment—to God, yourself, a supportive friend—or even the perpetrator if the Spirit leads you to do so. We must not allow our ego, pride, or fear to cause us to deny that we're feeling displeasure because our expectation has been dashed. I was recently disappointed and angered when a family member yelled at me and used profanity to boot. I never thought a blood relative would speak to me that way.

     King David was deeply disappointed that his efforts had yielded such disastrous results. We sense his frustration with God for such a harsh judgment for an apparently innocent act. "David was afraid of the LORD that day; and he said, 'How can the ark of the LORD come to me?'" (2 Samuel 6:9).

- Place a time limit on how long you will languish on the bed of disappointment. Yes, it's human to feel disappointed, but we cannot allow this emotion to set up permanent residence in our soul. To do so says to God, "I don't like what You have allowed. I still want my way." This can lead to disillusionment and bitterness.

Depending upon the nature of the disappointment, I'll often say to myself, *Okay, Deborah, you get X number of minutes/hours to grieve the death of your plan or expectation. You will not keep wishing it were different; you will move on. God has spoken.*

Caution: When you are disappointed because you are certain the outcome is contrary to God's will, keep standing in faith for the desired result. David didn't allow misfortune to kill his dream of bringing the ark to the capital city; he simply took time to regroup. "So David would not move the ark of the LORD with him into the City of David; but David took it aside into the house of Obed-Edom the Gittite. The ark of the LORD remained in the house of Obed-Edom the Gittite three months. And the LORD blessed Obed-Edom and all his household" (2 Samuel 6:10-11).

- Acknowledge any mistakes, miscommunication, or disobedience on your part that may have contributed to the disappointment. In analyzing the ark debacle, David realized he had not obeyed God's original instructions to Moses on how to transport the ark. They had made a gross error in placing the ark on an oxcart; it was to be carried only by poles on the shoulders of certain Levites (Numbers 4:1-6,15-20). Further, no one was to actually *touch* it except the qualifying priests. Thus, we learn that Uzzah's innocent reflex action in steadying the cart was an act of desecration.

• Ask God, "What now?" Maintaining a forward focus keeps you from getting stuck in frustration or anger over what could have been if only this or that had happened. Seek God for new instructions. Stay optimistic about a better outcome in the future. Before his next attempt to bring the ark to Jerusalem, David told the qualifying priests,

> "You are the heads of the fathers' houses of the Levites; sanctify yourselves...that you may bring up the ark of the LORD God of Israel to the place I have prepared for it. For because you did not do it the first time, the LORD our God broke out against us, because we did not consult Him about the proper order."
>
> So the priests and the Levites sanctified themselves to bring up the ark of the Lord God of Israel. And the children of the Levites bore the ark of God on their shoulders, by its poles, as Moses had commanded according to the word of the Lord (1 Chronicles 15:12-15).

The ark finally arrived in Jerusalem amidst great rejoicing (1 Chronicles 16). Mission accomplished!

- Accept every disappointment as "His-Appoint-ment." Although God may not have initiated the disappointing circumstance, He can surely turn it into something good. Therefore, look beyond the situation and believe that all things are work-ing together for your good because you love God and are called according to His purpose (Romans 8:28). Also, remember that God may not be can-celling your plans but rather postponing them for a divinely ordered time.

We will all experience disappointments. Overcom-ing them requires a mindset that is humble enough to submit to God's plan, flexible enough to extend His grace to others, and faithful enough to stay focused on the future.

Faith Declaration

I had plans and expectations, but God's purpose has prevailed. May He be glorified.

Day 10

Ripped Off

Do not say, "I'll pay you back for this wrong!"
Wait for the LORD, and he will avenge you.
PROVERBS 20:22 NIV

My friend Ann and her elderly father, Sam, were both frugal money managers. They also loved supporting the work of the Lord. Sam often made personal loans to small congregations in his hometown for their special building projects. When he passed away, one such loan was still outstanding even though the maturity date had expired. Sam had been smart enough to secure the $26,000 loan with a trust deed against the property that had an estimated market value of ten times more than the loan.

Ann, the executrix of his will, collected one payment from the pastor and asked him to propose whatever repayment terms were comfortable for the dwindling congregation. The pastor promised full repayment within six months; however, he never contacted Ann after that and refused to return her phone calls. Ann sent several letters asking for payment, but the pastor ignored them. Finally, she hired Lawyer X to foreclose. She advised him that she did not wish to see the congregation evicted from the property. Therefore, she wanted the estate to take ownership to assure their continued occupancy.

However, Lawyer X, seeing the significant profit potential, tipped off his real estate friend and advised him to place a bid at the auction of the property. Through a series of dishonest maneuvers, including sending the foreclosure notice to the wrong address as well as refusing to bid on behalf of the estate as Ann had instructed, Lawyer X successfully auctioned the property to his friend for the $26,000 debt.

Ann and her siblings were furious. They knew the very person hired to represent their interests had ripped them off. Lawyer X justified his actions by saying, "My goal was to make you 'whole' by recovering the amount owed to the estate; it was not to make you a profit by letting the building default to you."

Ann realized after several failed attempts to hire another local attorney to sue Lawyer X that the old boys' club would stick together. Suing each other was not part of their culture. Knowing that it would be unlikely to find a fair judge even if she hired a nonlocal attorney, Ann finally accepted that Lawyer X had ripped off the estate. She reported the incident to the state lawyers association and decided to get on with her life. The heirs are still stewing in their anger and plotting revenge.

Feeling ripped off can enrage us and make us devise evil ways to right the wrong. After all, something we have a right to, something of value has been ripped from us and, by golly, we want it back!

Consider how Jacob and his mother, Rebekah,

conspired to cheat Esau, the firstborn son, out of the official blessing from his father, Isaac (Genesis 27). Esau was a hairy hunter and Jacob was a smooth-skinned mama's boy. Notwithstanding, Rebekah successfully disguised Jacob (going as far as putting animal skin on his arms), and together they tricked the poor-sighted Isaac into pronouncing the blessing on Jacob. When Esau learned of the deception, he became furious. He plotted to avenge the wrong as soon as his father died: "So Esau hated Jacob because of the blessing with which his father blessed him, and Esau said in his heart, 'The days of mourning for my father are at hand; then I will kill my brother Jacob'" (27:41). Rebekah got wind of the plot and sent Jacob away to live with his Uncle Laban.

When you feel someone has ripped you off, try these strategies for staying on the right side of God and the local law:

- Take time to think soberly and to understand your options. Do not retaliate or take the law into your own hands. If you can find a remedy through a legal process, then pursue that route—especially if a significant amount is at stake.

- Take your complaint to the next level of authority. However, you may ultimately have to submit your ego and your anger to the reality of the situation and accept your loss. There comes a point when the time, cost, or frustrations just aren't worth it. Look for the lesson learned. This can be very hard, but the sooner you let it go, the more energy you can devote to bigger and better pursuits.

- Protect others from future rip-offs. Register your complaint with appropriate state boards and regulatory agencies, the Better Business Bureau (BBB.com), online sites such as FightBack.com, BadDealings.com, the SqueakyWheel.com, and other forums for disgruntled customers.

- Rest assured that perpetrators reap what they sow. Life was no picnic for Jacob as Laban constantly deceived him at every opportunity (Genesis 29–31).

Faith Declaration

I will honor God in responding to a rip-off, knowing that vengeance belongs to Him and that He is able to do exceedingly and abundantly above all I can ask or think according to His power that works in me (see Ephesians 3:20).

Day 11

Humiliated

*"We learn humility through accepting
humiliations cheerfully."*
MOTHER TERESA

King Ahasuerus made a big mistake. After seven
days of nonstop partying with the nobles and princes of
his 127 provinces, the drunken ruler got the bright idea
that his wife, Queen Vashti, should come and parade
herself in front of his male guests so they could behold
her beauty. "But when they conveyed the king's order
to Queen Vashti, she refused to come. This made the
king furious, and he burned with anger" (Esther 1:12
NLT). Vashti was obviously a woman of great modesty.
She was also courageous enough to stick by her personal
moral code.

Not sure how to deal with her rebellion, the humiliated king asked his inner circle of policy experts to weigh
in on the matter from the standpoint of the Persian law.
They warned him that tolerating Vashti's behavior would
set a bad precedent (1:13-20). Women throughout the
provinces would refuse to submit to their husbands
whether great or small. Disrespect would abound. They

counseled that the only face-saving solution would be to dethrone the queen and replace her with a specially selected, beautiful young virgin.

The king followed their advice, and in so doing, he paved the way for Esther, a Jewish girl who initially hid her ethnicity, to become queen and ultimately to use her influence to save her people from extermination.

Humiliation is one of the most painful emotions that anyone can experience. The word *humiliation* is derived from the Latin root word *humus*, which means "earth or soil," and the suffix *-ate*, meaning "cause to be." To humiliate literally means "cause to be soil"—or in modern terms, "to treat like dirt" or "to bring low." Few actions can rouse a person's anger more quickly than being made to feel "less than" or devalued.

One element of a humiliating experience that makes it so painful is the presence of witnesses. Most of us could probably handle an altercation, a put-down, or other ego-bruising encounter done in private. However, we hate for someone else to see us looking powerless or diminished in any way. That's why, in group settings, we may pretend to understand discussions or to comprehend matters that are way over our heads. We worry that others will judge us as intellectually inferior.

So we can understand why King Ahasuerus not only banished Vashti from her throne but also sent letters to all the provinces declaring "each man should be master in his own house" (Esther 1:22). How else could the powerful ruler of all of Persia protect his image after Vashti so blatantly proved him powerless to rule his own house?

Jesus was well acquainted with humiliation. The humbling facts of his U-shaped career path are best summarized by the apostle Paul in his letter to the Philippians:

Though he was God,
>> he did not think of equality with God
>> as something to cling to.
Instead, he gave up his divine privileges;
>> he took the humble position of a slave
>> and was born as a human being.
When he appeared in human form,
>> he humbled himself in obedience to God
>> and died a criminal's death on a cross.
Therefore, God elevated him to the place of
>> highest honor
>> and gave him the name above all other names,
that at the name of Jesus every knee should bow,
>> in heaven and on earth and under the earth,
and every tongue confess that Jesus Christ is Lord,
>> to the glory of God the Father.

> (Philippians 2:6-11 NLT)

In our fallen world, humiliation is usually met with a desire for revenge or retaliation. However, our sinless Savior entertained no such thoughts. At His crucifixion, He simply said, "Father, forgive them, for they do not know what they do" (Luke 23:34). If we claim to have the mind of Christ, we would be wise to use His model. Specifically, we would be wise to:

- Reframe the experience. Whether you've been insulted, your ego bruised, or you feel diminished, know that *everything* has a purpose—a good purpose when you love God. There are no useless pains or sorrows, so don't waste them. Immediately look for the lesson learned.

- Stop and ask yourself why you are giving so much power to the *observers* of your humiliation. You can't control what they will think of you. It's what *you* think of yourself that determines the extent of your emotional pain.

- Don't encourage continued humiliation by responding in a powerless manner. If someone rejects you, don't beg him to stay connected to you. Accept his decision and move on. If your boss humiliates you, calmly explain to him how his behavior affects your morale. Be clear on how you would prefer him to interact with you going forward.

Faith Declaration

Humiliation is my stepping-stone to a life of humility. The Holy Spirit empowers me to handle and to overcome all such experiences with grace and strength.

Day 12

Rejected

"Practice, practice, practice until you eventually get numb on rejections."
BRIAN KLEMMER, PERSONAL
DEVELOPMENT COACH

Rejection hurts, literally. Researchers call it social pain. A 2010 study suggested that our brain responds to social rejection with the same distress receptors as physical pain.[4] Rejection validates our feelings of inadequacy, inferiority, or worthlessness. It is now commonplace in American society.

The entertainment industry has packaged rejection into television programs that invite us to participate in determining winners and losers. Every week, Americans flip on their televisions to watch dozens of potential dream dates, singing sensation hopefuls, or even culinary contestants have their dreams dashed by celebrity judges or fellow show participants. We cast our text-message or phone-in votes to the latest brand of interactive reality show. Some of the contestants respond with tears and noted discouragement, while others get angry and criticize the judges or fellow contestants. The smart ones respond with gratitude for the opportunity and keep their priorities in perspective.

Though we get regular doses of watching others deal with their rejection, it does not lessen the impact on our minds, hearts, and bodies when we experience it ourselves. Once, Darnell and I visited a church where I was scheduled to speak in a few months. During the service, the assistant pastor asked each person to join with two other people to pray for one another's personal needs. I was impressed with the fervency of the prayer that an elderly woman in my group prayed.

After church, I turned to her and said, "It was a delight meeting you. Here is my card. Could I ask you to put me on your prayer list? I'll be speaking here in a few months at your conference."

"I'm afraid I can't do that," she replied as she refused to accept the card. "I have a huge list of people I have to pray for already, and it's getting to be too much."

I immediately felt rejected. Who would refuse to pray for the speaker? How much time does it take anyway to say, "God, bless the speaker"? Why, some people would consider it an honor to be asked! I smarted over the sting of her response for several hours. I found myself fretting about why she wouldn't make an exception for me. Then I decided to take my own advice:

- Respect other people's decision not to engage or continue in a relationship with you. Surely, there has been a time in your life when you have made a similar choice. It was simply a personal decision.

- Don't agonize over *why* the person or group made the decision. Sometimes circumstances dictate that they tell you no; the timing, the limited resources, or other issues may not be conducive to a yes. (The prayer warrior who rejected me obviously takes prayer requests very seriously and earnestly prays over them versus some who say they will pray and forget all about it or just never find the time to do so.)

  In a job situation, you might ask what you could do to get a yes in the future. If the rejection causes you to discover a better way to do something, thank God for the lesson. Otherwise, accept it as part of your divine destiny. When dealing with romantic relationships, view rejection as His protection.

- Keep your joy. Each time I'm disappointed, I sing aloud the chorus to "I Still Have Joy" by gospel singer Dorothy Norwood, which speaks of still having joy in spite of going through difficult circumstances.[5] The strength to maintain my joy usually comes as I choose to sing rather than entertain negative thoughts about the rejection.

- Hold on to your confidence. When your internal sense of security is threatened, you create space in your heart and mind for anger to control your actions. Remember you do not have immunity from rejection.

  Besides, you are in good company. Jesus was

rejected and abandoned but never responded with anger: "He came to His own, and His own did not receive Him" (John 1:11); "then all the disciples forsook Him and fled" (Matthew 26:56). He even felt abandoned by His heavenly Father as He hung on the cross, carrying the sins of the world: "My God, My God, why have You forsaken me?" (Matthew 27:46).

Faith Declaration

I am accepted by my Father who will never leave me nor forsake me. Neither rejection, nor abandonment, nor any social pain will separate me from His love. He has allowed every circumstance that comes into my life and everything is working together for my good.

Day 13

Manipulated

*Let every man be fully persuaded
in his own mind.*
ROMANS 14:5B KJV

Manipulative people want one thing: to control your behavior to achieve their personal objectives. If you have fallen into the clutches of a manipulator, she targeted you because she perceived you as weak, needy, vulnerable, inexperienced, less spiritual, naïve, fearful, and a host of other negatives. However, before we grab our sticks to beat manipulators, let's remember that we all have a tendency to manipulate others. Since manipulation is such a broad area of concern, let me hasten to highlight some common tactics that manipulators use.

Flattery. Insincere compliments will work every time if you don't have a strong sense of your personal worth. "Oh, you are the sweetest member at that church," someone might say. Later, they may ask, "Can you lend me $100 until the first of the month?"

Guilt. When Delilah agreed to betray Samson (Judges 16), she pouted and ran a guilt trip on him until she wore him down. "Then she said to him, 'How can you say, "I love you," when your heart is not with me? You have mocked me these three times, and have not told me where your great strength lies'" (16:15). Well, you know the end of the story. She shaved his head, and poof went his strength. Only God knows how many young boys and men have used this same "If you loved me you would…" tactic and manipulated their girlfriends into having premarital sex or extending other favors.

Deceit/Lies. Jezebel, wife of King Ahab, was the queen of Israel; she was also the queen of manipulation. When Ahab pouted because Naboth, his next-door neighbor, wouldn't sell him his vineyard so Ahab could plant a vegetable garden, Jezebel took matters into her own hands. She paid men to testify that Naboth had blasphemed God and the king—a crime punishable by death. After Naboth was stoned to death, Jezebel told Ahab to take possession of the vineyard. (Read the entire spellbinding story and Jezebel's tragic end at 1 Kings 21 and 2 Kings 9.)

Threats. Sally, now in her fifties and fearing that her best days are behind her, tolerates untold verbal abuse from her new husband, Wally. When there is a conflict between them, he threatens to leave the marriage. Fearing loneliness, she caves in to his wishes; however, each time she does so, she resents herself for being so needy and for empowering him to be an even stronger manipulator.

Generosity. Okay, I confess that I've been the manipulator and the manipulated on this one. It's so easy to use generosity as a carrot to obligate people. How dare they say no after all we've done for them? We must really guard our hearts on this one to keep our motives pure. To avoid the clutches of a manipulator, be wary of gifts that might have strings attached. If you are single, it's wise to refuse extravagant gifts from the opposite sex.

Anger/Silent treatment. People who have a reputation for being angry all the time, or are easily provoked to anger, use this emotion to manipulate people into submitting to their desires. The average person wants peace in their environment. An angry person pollutes the atmosphere and spoils the fun—much like a skunk at a picnic. Therefore, to appease them, most will go along to get along to preserve the peace. Unfortunately, caving in to the angry person's wishes only reinforces their behavior. Further, you now start to develop self-loathing for allowing yourself to be victimized.

Playing the victim. This one is self-explanatory: "Everybody treats me unfairly." "I'm an old lady now and I guess I'm just in the way." Don't fall for this trap!

Unreasonable requests. Manipulators may ask you for something unreasonable before asking for what they really want. Teens are masters at this. "Dad, may I have $300 to buy a pair of hot new tennis shoes? Oh, I can't have that? Then how about $25 so I can at least go to the movies with my friends?" Employees often use this tactic also. They may request a huge unmerited raise when what they really want is a Christmas bonus or an extra week of vacation.

To avoid becoming a manipulator's unwitting prey, try these strategies:

- "To thine own self be true." Practice self-awareness and know which tactics you are most vulnerable to. I have found it hard to say no to someone who has been generous to me, even though I may have suspected an ulterior motive in the first place. I usually will graciously refuse the gift or find a way to reciprocate to keep from being indebted to a potential manipulator.

- Avoid people who pressure you to make choices that you don't prefer. If the manipulator is someone you have frequent interaction with, assert your stance. "Listen, I'm a person with strong individual preferences. It's futile to try to persuade me against my will." Be a broken record.

- Readily admit the role you played in facilitating a manipulator's triumph. This will keep you from repeating negative patterns and from getting stuck thinking you are a totally innocent victim.

- Reinforce your boundaries—the guidelines you establish for how other people must interact with you. Boundaries clarify for the people in your circle of interaction behaviors you consider acceptable or unacceptable. You honor your relationships by keeping people from having to guess how you may interpret their actions. In an ideal world, they would also communicate their boundaries.

   Now, this is not about people sitting down with their individual "rule books" and laying down the law. More often, it's about sensing situations before—or even when—they arise and communicating your druthers or preferences in a calm, confident manner.

- Don't get angry, get wise. In his book, *Don't Waste Your Sorrows*, the late Paul Billheimer admonished his readers not to waste the benefits and lesson of problems and adversities. Consider how you can use incidents of potential manipulation to learn more about yourself and the perpetrator.

- Don't confuse manipulation with genuine concern. Parents may try subtle and not-so-subtle tactics to control their children's romantic involvements or career preferences. A key question to ask yourself is, *Who will benefit most if I pursue the suggested action?* Remember that manipulators have *selfish* motives and are not looking out for your best interests. Ask God to reveal the real motives.

- Don't stay on high alert for manipulation. Give, serve, and sacrifice as you have purposed in your heart and don't mar your joy wondering if you were manipulated into doing so.

Faith Declaration

I can easily discern manipulating tactics and have the courage to resist falling prey to controlling people.

Day 14

Accused

"No weapon formed against you shall prosper,
And every tongue which rises
against you in judgment
You shall condemn.
This is the heritage of the servants of the Lord,
And their righteousness is from Me,"
Says the Lord.
Isaiah 54:17

The rollercoaster of Joseph's life was about to take another downward plunge. He had once enjoyed an exalted family position as his father's favorite son. Unfortunately, his envious brothers sold him into slavery. Potiphar, an Egyptian official, purchased him and showed him great favor. He put Joseph in charge of his entire household. When Mrs. Potiphar made sexual advances toward Joseph, the handsome, trustworthy, and godly Israelite fled from her. In the play *The Mourning Bride*, playwright William Congreve (1670–1729) says, "Heaven has no rage like love to hatred turned, nor hell a fury like a woman scorned." He was right. The scorned Mrs. Potiphar falsely accused Joseph of attempted rape.

Upon hearing the charge, her husband threw him into the king's prison.

A false accusation will quickly provoke anger in most people. But not Joseph. He asserted his innocence but maintained a great attitude. The prison keeper put him in charge of all the other prisoners. Joseph didn't know it, but everything was happening according to a divine plan. He befriended a fellow prisoner who happened to be the king's butler. He also interpreted the butler's dream and told him that Pharaoh would restore him to his position. It all happened as Joseph said.

Two years later, when Pharaoh had a disturbing dream, the butler remembered that Joseph had accurately interpreted his dream and told Pharaoh about him. So Pharaoh sent for Joseph, who explained to him that a severe economic downturn was about to occur. Joseph also gave him a strategy to minimize the damage. Pharaoh appointed him to be second in charge of the entire land of Egypt to manage the situation. (You can read the entire saga of Joseph's trials and triumphs in Genesis 37 and 39–50.)

We are all prone to falling prey to the unfair and potentially damaging accusations or misjudgments of others. Sometimes when it happens to us, the flames of fury are easily ignited with righteous indignation. Such difficult circumstances demand that we control our attitudes and our tempers as they can leave devastating wounds with lasting scars.

Perhaps you can identify with such an experience. Maybe someone you thought was your friend spread a false rumor. Or maybe you have gone through a painful divorce and experienced the harsh opinions or judgments of others. Many have been falsely accused and convicted of crimes they did not commit. Even Jesus was subjected to false accusations and constantly attacked by the judgmental leaders of His time. Yet He loved, forgave, and died for His accusers.

Accusations contain the power of deceit, the force of malice, and the fuel of anger. They can erode your confidence, your ability to trust, and your faith in humanity. When you face accusations, try these God-honoring responses:

- Stay calm and don't become exasperated with the person or group making the accusation.

- Rather than becoming indignant, try to find out what caused the accuser to believe that you are guilty as charged. Some accusations are born out of wrong perceptions of your behavior.

- Connect with supportive family members, friends, or coworkers who have faced similar circumstances to get their wisdom and encouragement on surviving the ordeal. Stay away from those who are still bitter about their experience.

- If you have factual, objective information that will refute the accusation, by all means present it. When I was accused of misinterpreting my deceased father's will and not disclosing all of his assets, I made all financial records available to the heirs. I also submitted legal opinions I had solicited from other attorneys. The matter was finally squashed. Also, if there is a credible witness or someone who can corroborate your story, ask her to do so.

- Even if you prove the accusations are false, release any expectations that the accuser *must* apologize. Forgive him anyway; apologies are not prerequisites for forgiveness. Don't allow intrusive thoughts of injustice to torment you into a bitter existence. Rather, meditate on Scriptures that speak of God avenging the wrongs perpetrated on us. The following passage has comforted me during such difficult times:

> Do not take revenge, my dear friends, but leave room for God's wrath, for it is written: "It is mine to avenge; I will repay," says the Lord…Do not be overcome by evil, but overcome evil with good (Romans 12:19,21 NIV).

Faith Declaration

Every word spoken against me shall be judged by my heavenly Father, who will quickly avenge my adversaries.

Day 15

Disadvantaged

*"The man who thinks he can and the man
who thinks he can't are both right."*
HENRY FORD

Gabrielle (Gabby) Douglas, the artistic gymnast
and member of the U.S. women's gymnastics team at
the 2012 Summer Olympics, won gold medals in both
the individual and team all-around competitions. She is
the first African-American in Olympic history to win the
individual all-around competition. The sixteen-year-old
Gabby had triumphed over separation from her family,
relocating at age fourteen from Virginia Beach, Virginia,
to live with a white host family in West Des Moines,
Iowa, to train under a special coach. She also had to overcome financial hardship and racism. While the racism
cut her to the core, she did not allow anger to pierce
her soul. Despite her circumstances, she never saw herself as disadvantaged. In a subsequent TV interview, she
described her victory as "a God thing." Indeed it was.

During Jesus's short time on the earth, He demonstrated His special affinity for the disadvantaged people of His day. In fact, when Herod Antipas had John

the Baptist thrown into prison for speaking out against Herod's marriage to his own brother's former wife, John began to doubt whether Jesus really was the Messiah. Therefore, he sent messengers to ask Jesus the big question: "Are You the Coming One, or do we look for another?" (Luke 7:19). Jesus responded, "Go and tell John the things you have seen and heard: that the blind see, the lame walk, the lepers are cleansed, the deaf hear, the dead are raised, the poor have the gospel preached to them" (Luke 7:22).

Wow! What a list of the disadvantaged: the disabled, the social outcasts, and the impoverished. He came to give them all abundant life in Him.

Society, special interest groups, and others have subjected generations of men and women to social disadvantage because of selfish intents or biased ideas. Anger is often evoked with a ripple effect upon many in such situations. The person being disadvantaged, as well as the person whose advantage is then threatened, may become angry and begin a cycle of rage. When we cling to the belief that we are disadvantaged, we can easily give our minds over to both fear and anger—and ultimately resentment and bitterness.

Here are a few strategies that will keep you focused in the right direction and maintain your peace:

- Read the biographies or highlights of the lives of others who share your particular disadvantage. The next time you decide that life is not fair or that you have been handed the short end of the stick, consider the victories of the following people:

> *Mephibosheth,* the son of Jonathan (David's best friend), was crippled in both feet as a result of a fall. Such a handicap would have made him a social outcast. However, when David became king, he searched him out to favor him due to his commitment to take care of the now-deceased Jonathan's household. Mephibosheth was privileged to sit at the king's table daily (2 Samuel 9).

> *Louis Braille,* a French educator, was blind and invented the Braille system of printing with raised dots to enable blind people to read.

> *Thomas A. Edison,* the "father of electricity," was hearing impaired and had learning disabilities. He was relentless in his quest to develop a practical lightbulb along with an electrical system to support it. He overcame failure hundreds if not thousands of times to accomplish his goal.

> *Kyle Maynard* was born with arms that end at the elbows and legs near the knees. In his bestselling memoir *No Excuses*, he tells how he overcame physical disadvantages to become a champion in wrestling and in life.

Oprah Winfrey turned a life of hardship into inspiration for a multibillion-dollar empire. The Oprah name became a brand. In 2011, *Forbes* magazine estimated her net worth at $2.7 billion.

The one thing all these disadvantaged people had in common was their belief that they could overcome their obstacles, hardships, and physical disabilities. Russell Simmons, entrepreneur and record producer, says "There are no failures, only quitters." If you are frustrated or angry about what you deem an impossible hurdle you must overcome, try these strategies:

- Adopt a divine perspective when you experience feelings of deprivation or disadvantage. Remind yourself that you have a specific destiny that no one can thwart. "For the LORD Almighty has purposed, and who can thwart him? His hand is stretched out, and who can turn it back?" (Isaiah 14:27 NIV).

- Pray specific Scriptures over your circumstances. (*Hint:* To find related passages, go to www .Google.com and type in the search box "Scriptures about" (blindness, disabilities, etc.) or "what the Bible says about." Know that your adversity is a character builder and can produce great rewards. Therefore, start thanking God for His blessings even before they are revealed.

- Abandon the use of the term *disadvantaged* when speaking of your circumstances or position in life—even if you are disabled, bereft of finances, or from a family of low social status. Labeling yourself as disadvantaged is a self-fulfilling prophecy. You may have to overcome a few more obstacles than the average person, but you are never disadvantaged if you are connected to the all-powerful (omnipotent), all-knowing (omniscient), and everywhere-present (omnipresent) God.

Faith Declaration

God saw me before I was born. Every day of my life was recorded in His book. Every moment was laid out before a single day had passed (see Psalm 139:16 NLT). And since "God shows personal favoritism to no man" (Galatians 2:6), nothing and no one can block my destiny.

Day 16

Unappreciated

"Whoever desires to become great among you shall be your servant."
MARK 10:43

One day as Jesus was entering a certain village, ten lepers cried out to Him to heal them. Without stating that He would grant their request, He simply told them to go and present themselves to the priest (as required by ceremonial law). As they went to do so, they suddenly realized that they had been healed.

However, only one of them returned to express his gratitude for his healing. "So Jesus answered and said, 'Were there not ten cleansed? But where are the nine? Were there not any found who returned *to give glory to God* except this foreigner?'" (Luke 17:17-18). Even Jesus experienced what it was like to extend kindness to others only to have them take it for granted. Although it obviously displeased Him, Jesus didn't allow the lepers' ingratitude to move Him to anger. He had healed them strictly for the glory of God. He simply marveled that they could take God's goodness so lightly. Most ingrates never stop to recognize the hand of God in others extending kindness to them.

I'm tired of ungrateful people. When I give my time, resources, and other forms of benevolence to people, and they act as if they were entitled to it, I have to ask God for special grace to deal with my frustration. I usually attribute their behavior to lack of home training or just poor people skills. However, I'm more disappointed with myself. I want my first response to their ingratitude to be, "It's okay. I did it for God's glory anyway." I confess it is not. Why, I've been known to call a few recipients (usually relatives and close friends) and say, "Hey, where is my thank you card for that gift?"

What about you? Do you often find yourself in situations where you feel that people take your service, sacrifices, gifts, or other acts of kindness for granted? Are you frustrated or angered by it? If so, try these tactics to overcome feeling unappreciated:

- Evaluate your real motive for extending the kindness in the first place. Are you really doing it as Jesus did, that is, for God's glory? Or are you seeking your own glory in the form of accolades, acceptance, or access to those who can reciprocate in various ways? When we serve with selfish intentions, we are bound to encounter selfish people who take us for granted.

- Employee, if you are overloaded with responsibilities, talk to your boss and determine if you are indeed carrying a disproportionate share of the workload. Ask her how she plans to reward you (I'm assuming you are excellent at your job).

If she has no plans, then propose *your* plan for a bonus, extended time off, or other compensation. Try to keep your request within the confines of your company's policies and culture. If less work is what you desire, then consider requesting a reduced work schedule after prayerfully evaluating your household budget. By the way, "no" works when fellow employees try to dump their work on you.

- Wife/mother, if your husband takes you for granted and doesn't do his fair share of household responsibilities, maybe you have taught him that it's okay to treat you this way. Perhaps you have been taught some dysfunctional coping strategies, including suffering in silence. As a result, your anger goes underground, turns into resentment and bitterness, and destroys your relationship.

  This is not a call to rebellion. However, if you have already discussed the problem but your husband continues to ignore you, ask God to show you what consequences you can implement that would not be dishonoring to the marriage or your faith. You may have to let go of some of your "neat freak" ways to drive your point home.

  This is a hot issue in a lot of marriages and calm, effective communication is critical. You will feel a lot more peaceful if you and your husband negotiate specific responsibilities for him to assume. Stay cordial, loving, and hopeful of a positive outcome. Further, commit to maintaining your mental health by scheduling times to socialize with others. Do as the airlines warn before every flight—"secure your oxygen mask first" if others are depending on you for assistance. This is going to make you a better wife and mother. Now, don't forget to acknowledge and express appreciation for any progress your husband makes.

- Relatives/employer/others, if ungrateful people in your circle continue to diminish the quality of your life, let them know how their behavior is affecting you. Remember you have a choice to continue, reduce, or stop the services or sacrifices that you are making. Just continue to monitor your motives. "If your gift is to encourage others, be encouraging. If it is giving, give generously. If God has given you leadership ability, take the responsibility seriously. And if you have a gift for showing kindness to others, do it gladly. Don't just pretend to love others. Really love them" (Romans 12:8-9 NLT).

Faith Declaration

I serve others with a pure motive and accept responsibilities only as God leads.

Day 17

Powerless

"O LORD, God of our ancestors, you alone are
the God who is in heaven. You are ruler of all
the kingdoms of the earth. You are powerful
and mighty; no one can stand against you!"

2 CHRONICLES 20:6-7 NLT

Rachel wanted to bear a child more than anything in the world. Her husband, Jacob, who would later become the patriarch of the twelve tribes of Israel, loved her dearly. In fact, he agreed to work for her father Laban for seven years in exchange for her hand in marriage (Genesis 29). Unfortunately, the unscrupulous Laban pulled a fast one at the end of the term. On the night of the wedding, he had Rachel's older, less attractive sister Leah go into the marriage bed instead of Rachel.

Jacob was furious but powerless to do anything about the situation. Knowing that Jacob was madly in love with Rachel, Laban negotiated to give her to him the following week if he agreed to work another seven years. Jacob finally had the woman of his dreams. He loved her exclusively. Seeing Leah was unloved, God made her fruitful, and she had several children while Rachel endured the social stigma of being barren. Rachel pestered Jacob to do something about her plight:

> Now when Rachel saw that she bore Jacob no children, Rachel envied her sister, and said to Jacob, "Give me children, or else I die!"
>
> And Jacob's anger was aroused against Rachel, and he said, "Am I in the place of God, who has with held from you the fruit of the womb?" (Genesis 30:1-2).

Jacob was frustrated that he was powerless to impregnate Rachel. However, in God's timing, Rachel gave birth to Joseph (Genesis 30:22-24) and Benjamin (Genesis 35:17-18), who became Jacob's favorite sons.

Whether we are stuck in traffic, an elevator, a bad relationship, a declining neighborhood, a dead-end job, or any other situation we think we have no way of changing, feelings of powerlessness can easily turn into anger. Anger gives us a false sense of empowerment. Someone once said, "Anger is how we attempt to reassert control over situations that baffle us."

This may sound like doublespeak but, spiritually, there is great power in our powerlessness for this is the place where God demonstrates His power best. When the apostle Paul was plagued with a weakness, he sought God three times to remove it from him. God refused to do so. He simply replied, "My grace is sufficient for you, for My strength is made perfect in weakness" (2 Corinthians 12:9).

Rather than dwelling on how awful your situation is or hiding behind the wall of blaming others, start taking personal responsibility for getting God's direction for making a change. He is going to use *you* to solve *your* problem. You are never powerless when His Spirit dwells within you. God is "able to do exceedingly abundantly above all that we ask or think, according to the *power that works in us*" (Ephesians 3:20). So, here is a plan for getting out of the pit of powerlessness:

- Acknowledge your powerlessness to God as an act of surrender to His will and purpose for your situation. Read how King Jehoshaphat triumphed over three powerful armies when he prayed this prayer: "O our God, won't you stop them? We are powerless against this mighty army that is about to attack us. We do not know what to do, but we are looking to you for help" (2 Chronicles 20:12 NLT).

- Don't whine to others about being powerless. Doing so will sabotage your faith to believe for a miracle and minimize your courage to pursue the solution God wants to reveal to you. This is also a good time to abandon any illusions about being in control of those other areas of your life that seem to be going well. We do not control *anything*. Everything good that is happening to us is all by the grace of God.

- Shed your "victim robe" and be honest about your role in the problem. Stop placing the blame on others. Prayerfully determine what empowering action you can take now to begin making a difference in your situation (saying no, confronting an offender, being honest about your desires and expectations, setting boundaries, getting better equipped or trained). Don't let fear of other people's reactions or rejection paralyze you from moving forward. You are more valuable than you think. Besides, you have powerful friends in high places—the Father, the Son, and the Holy Spirit!

I know I've been a little hard on you in this chapter, but I sense you need to be snatched out of your lethargy so you can start living the abundant life Jesus died for you to have.

Faith Declaration

The power of God that dwells in me is enabling me to triumph in every situation.

Day 18

Depressed

Why am I discouraged?
Why is my heart so sad?
I will put my hope in God!
I will praise him again—
my Savior and my God!
Now I am deeply discouraged,
but I will remember you.
Psalm 42:5-6 NLT

The prophet Elijah went from the mountaintop to the valley—physically and emotionally. His spiritual exploits were renowned. Why, by God's power, he had even raised a widow's son from the dead (1 Kings 17:17-24). He humiliated 450 false prophets when he challenged them to a miraculous demonstration to compare the power of Baal with the power of God (1 Kings 18:16-40). Their god failed, and Elijah ordered the people to kill every single one of them (verse 40). The showdown sparked a national revival. The Baal-worshipping Queen Jezebel was livid. How dare Elijah destroy her prophets! She sent word to Elijah that she would surely retaliate by taking his life the next day.

Elijah was afraid and fled for his life. He went to Beer-sheba, a town in Judah, and he left his servant there. Then he went on alone into the wilderness, traveling all day. He sat down under a solitary broom tree and prayed that he might die. "I have had enough, LORD," he said. "Take my life, for I am no better than my ancestors who have already died" (1 Kings 19:3-4 NLT).

Elijah was tired of fighting. His spirits were so low, this powerful man of God prayed to die.

Depression is an equal opportunity attacker. Nobody, great or small, is immune to its clutches. We all feel sad from time to time due to circumstances such as the death of a loved one, loss of a job, or the ending of a desired relationship. Mental health professionals make a distinction between short-term and long-term (clinical) depression. Here's the scoop according to Mayo Clinic psychiatrist, Daniel K. Hall-Flavin:

> Depression ranges in seriousness from mild, tempo-rary episodes of sadness to severe, persistent depres-sion. Doctors use the term "clinical depression" to describe the more severe form of depression also known as "major depression"...Clinical depression symptoms may include:
>
> • Depressed mood most of the day, nearly every day
>
> • Loss of interest or pleasure in most activities
>
> • Significant weight loss or gain
>
> • Sleeping too much or not being able to sleep nearly every day

- Slowed thinking or movement that others can see

- Fatigue or low energy nearly every day

- Feelings of worthlessness or inappropriate guilt

- Loss of concentration or indecisiveness

- Recurring thoughts of death or suicide

To meet the criteria for clinical depression…you must have five or more of the above symptoms over a two-week period. At least one of the symptoms must be either a depressed mood or a loss of interest or pleasure.[6]

Depression affects millions of people throughout the world. It can stem from chemical, genetic, environmental, or circumstantial factors. When in this state, the chemical messengers in the brain (primarily serotonin, the "feel good" chemical) run low and prevent nerve cells from communicating effectively. Perhaps this accounts for the unexplained anger. (See further discussion in chapter 29, "Chemical Imbalances.") It's important to recognize when depression is rearing its head in your life so that you can take timely steps to address it.

Unfortunately, many people treat their depression by self-medicating with all the wrong choices. They complicate their already problematic emotions with depressants such as drugs and alcohol that often aggravate the condition. Fortunately, God sent an angel to minister to Elijah, and after a period of resting and eating, he was back in the saddle (1 Kings 19).

Here are some practical and spiritual methods of

dealing with depression and defeating its power to turn you into Angry Annie or Terrible Tom.

- Recognize the symptoms (see above); don't rationalize them away.

- Don't delay in getting help. Research shows that the longer you wait, the more damage can be done. Cast down the notion that seeking help is a sign of weakness. It is actually an act of courage and wisdom to pursue a solution to a problem and improve the quality of your life.

- Don't go it alone. Isolation is one of the enemy's favorite weapons. Join a support group or prayer group to meet others who are also dealing with depression. Be accountable and grant a close friend or family member permission to monitor your progress.

  > Two are better than one,
  > Because they have a good reward for their labor.
  > For if they fall, one will lift up his companion.
  > But woe to him who is alone when he falls,
  > For he has no one to help him up.
  >   (Ecclesiastes 4:9-10).

- Get adequate rest. Chronic exhaustion can throw your brain chemicals into a tailspin. *Caution:* Do not use excessive sleep as an escape hatch to keep from dealing with the pain of depression.

- Eat wholesome foods (fresh fruits, vegetables, and lean protein); avoid products made with refined sugar and flour.

- Step up your exercise program. Physical activity is critical as it increases the production of serotonin.

- Engage in an activity you once enjoyed.

- Expect to get better and better each day.

Faith Declaration

God has plans for me. They are plans of peace and not of evil, to give me a future and a hope (Jeremiah 29:11).

Day 19

Disregarded

It is God who avenges me.
Psalm 18:47

It was more than just a perceived slight; it was a military misunderstanding that almost caused a civil war between two Jewish tribes. God had given Gideon specific instructions on how to defeat the Midianites, Israel's enemy. Through a series of miracles, Gideon and his specially selected army of three hundred triumphed over multiple thousands of men (Judges 7–8). But one of their fellow tribes, the Ephraimites, heard of their conquest and were furious that Gideon had not asked them to join the war since the Midianites were their common enemy. In fact, as the Midianites fled from Gideon and his men, the Ephraimites captured and killed two Midianite princes—a major triumph (7:25). Then they confronted Gideon about the perceived slight.

> Now the men of Ephraim said to him, "Why have you done this to us by not calling us when you went to fight with the Midianites?" And they reprimanded him sharply.
> So he said to them, "What have I done now in

comparison with you?…God has delivered into your hands the princes of Midian, Oreb and Zeeb. And what was I able to do in comparison with you?" Then their anger toward him subsided when he said that (Judges 8:1-3).

The right words…said at the right time…in the right manner. Gideon knew that a soft answer turns away wrath. Had it not been for his humble and gracious response, the story would likely have had a different ending.

Being disregarded by someone can deprive us of one of our most basic, universal human needs: the need for significance. When someone ignores us, the message we receive is, "You don't matter. I deem your presence, your input, your contribution to be of no consequence." Anger is a common response to such a slight.

Such was the case with John, an African-American who was traveling in the Deep South on a cross-country drive from California. When he entered the small country store, the white clerk was on the telephone and continued to talk without acknowledging John's presence. Several minutes later, another customer entered the store. He was white. The clerk immediately hung up the phone and asked him, "How can I help you?" After he completed the transaction, he finally asked John, "What do you want?"

"Nothing!" John yelled as he stormed out the door, slamming it so hard it threatened to fall from the hinges. He hopped into his car and sped down the highway like a madman. The highway patrol officer who pulled him over ten minutes later clocked his speed at ninety-five miles per hour. His response to being disregarded that day would cost him a lot of money and much delay as the fine had to be paid immediately to a local magistrate.

Now before I advise you on how to keep your peace when you are disregarded, ignored, snubbed, or otherwise treated as if you don't exist, let me caution you to examine your history in dealing with perceived slights. If you've had frequent occurrences, could it be that you are supersensitive to rejection and see a slight under every rock? Were you made to feel "less than" during your formative years to the point where you assume everybody looks for ways to keep you out of their circle of interaction?

Surely you've met people whose conversation is laden with such tales of rejection. When I encounter such a person, I too want to minimize my social interaction with them. But if this is not your history, protect your peace of mind in these situations by doing the following:

- Give the snubber the benefit of the doubt. Consider whether you really have been snubbed. Sometimes people are so preoccupied, they may not be aware of your presence or availability. So, go ahead and initiate the interaction and watch their response. At least you will be better able to judge their intentions.

- If you determine that you are genuinely being disregarded, take a deep breath and call immediately for heavenly backup. *I need you, Lord. Right now. Help me.* Reject any thoughts of retaliation or revenge.

- Make a commitment to yourself that you will never give such victimizers the power to invalidate your self-worth or to steal your joy. Further, do not assume that their snub is your problem. It could be that your presence reminds them of their own fears, failures, or unmet goals.

- If you can do so in a calm, nonemotional manner, confront the perpetrator. "Sally, I sense there is a problem here. Have I done something to offend you?" Don't sound as if you are pleading to be accepted and validated. You are simply getting information and giving your victimizer the benefit of the doubt.

- Remember the times that you have disregarded or ignored the Holy Spirit when He has spoken to your heart and instructed you to pursue or to refrain from a certain course of action. Understand that He is grieved (Ephesians 4:30) when we ignore Him. Yet, He doesn't cut us off. He keeps loving us and offering us guidance for our lives. Likewise, we must extend the same grace to others that He extends to us.

Faith Declaration

The Holy Spirit never leaves me. Because of Him, the fruit of self-control is manifested in me right now, giving me the power to respond to slights with grace and humility.

Day 20

Invaded

"Personal space refers to an area with invisible boundaries surrounding a person's body into which intruders may not come."
ROBERT SOMMER, ENVIRONMENTAL PSYCHOLOGIST

The airline personnel announced that my connecting flight from Houston to Los Angeles would be delayed for several hours. I was so disappointed and exhausted that I just plopped down on a seat in the waiting area and rested my head on the back of it. I was completely unaware that my rather bouffant hairdo was touching the neck of the man sitting in the seat behind me. He responded to the intrusion by simply saying, in a very even tone, "Excuse me." I was horrified that I had invaded his personal space. I apologized profusely. Of all people, I should have been more sensitive. After all, I'm always annoyed when someone trespasses into the space I've decided is my personal bubble. These trespasses include the following behaviors:

- standing too closely to me in a checkout line

- reaching across me in an elevator instead of asking me to press the number for their floor

- placing their items on the conveyor belt at the grocery store before I finish unloading my cart

- putting a purse or briefcase on my office desk without asking permission

- taking the seat right next to me in a waiting area where there are plenty of other empty seats

I'm sure you could add a few "space peeves" to this list since most people—especially Americans—value their personal space and feel uncomfortable, anxious, or violated when it is encroached.

Research has revealed four different zones of interpersonal space:

1. *Intimate* distance ranges from touching to about eighteen inches apart, and is reserved for lovers, children, as well as close family members and friends, and pets.

2. *Personal* distance begins about eighteen inches from the person and ends about four feet away. This space is used in conversations with friends, to chat with associates, and in group discussions.

3. *Social* distance ranges from four to eight feet from the person and is reserved for strangers, newly formed groups, and new acquaintances.

4. *Public* distance includes anything more than eight feet away and is used for speeches, lectures, and theater. Public distance is essentially that range reserved for larger audiences.[7]

People respond to intrusions of personal space in different ways. Some simply fume, some confront in a nonthreatening manner, and others respond with aggression. How do we as God's children maintain our peace of mind in the midst of such annoyances?

- Follow Jesus's example. Crowds thronged Him everywhere He went, constantly invading His personal space. "And the whole multitude sought to touch Him, for power went out from Him and healed them all" (Luke 6:19). He took it all in stride. When the woman with the issue of blood touched the hem of His robe, He questioned His disciples about who had done so. "His disciples said to him, 'Look at this crowd pressing around you. How can you ask, "Who touched me?"'" (Mark 5:31 NLT). His goal was to determine the identity of one with so much faith—not to rebuke her for getting too close.

- Speak up to get relief from annoying behavior that may continue. I had great respect for how my airport friend, with only two words, communicated his displeasure in a nonhostile way. Now, if someone is invading your space and you really think you are about to blow your stack, take a deep breath and kindly say, "I'm sorry. I need a little more space here."

- Be merciful. Remember that various cultures define personal space differently. Even if the offender is not from another culture, simply overlooking some incidents will help you guard your peace of mind. "A person's wisdom yields patience; it is to one's glory to overlook an offense" (Proverbs 19:11 NIV). There is a 99 percent chance that the space violator has no ill motives.

Faith Declaration

I walk in love toward all people. I have great peace because I love the law of God and nothing shall offend me (Psalm 119:165).

Day 21

Criticized

If you listen to constructive criticism,
you will be at home among the wise.
PROVERBS 15:31 NLT

"I use psychology on her and only tell her how wonderful she is," the junior executive confessed to me about the head of a key department in her organization. "She now confides in me. I know that she can't handle any kind of feedback, so I don't give her any. It works out better this way."

Such scenarios occur daily in businesses, charities, and families as many look for ways to cope with insecure leaders, coworkers, relatives, and others who view criticism—even when it is constructive—as a personal attack.

When I accepted an executive position at a major nonprofit many years ago, one of the first things I told my staff was that they would get brownie points for all constructive feedback. I further advised them that I had great disdain for cowardly people who chose instead to gossip or complain about the department's problems. Strong language, but it worked.

I'd found a great role model in Moses the Deliverer, and I wanted to emulate his attitude and his results. Two shining examples of his wise handling of feedback or criticism stand out during the Israelites' pilgrimage to the Promised Land. When Jethro, his father-in-law, came to visit him in the wilderness (Exodus 18), Jethro immediately noted Moses's ineffective administrative system for counseling the people. Long lines and frustration were the norm. Jethro suggested a structure whereby "rulers of thousands, rulers of hundreds, rulers of fifties, and rulers of tens" (verse 21) could help lighten his load. Not the least bit offended, the humble Moses "heeded the voice of his father-in-law and did all that he had said" (verse 24). When his older brother Aaron and his sister Miriam criticized him for marrying an Ethiopian woman, he ignored them, but God didn't. He struck Miriam with leprosy. Moses prayed for her and God healed her (Numbers 12). Neither constructive nor destructive criticism caused Moses to respond negatively.

I'm convinced that one of my divine callings is to give necessary feedback to leaders and difficult people. It is not an assignment I relish. Unlike Moses, some people get upset and do not receive it well. Many of those in authority have created a "compliments only" culture and view such feedback as a sign of disloyalty or as a personal attack.

Such was the case with King Asa. Hanani the seer told him in no uncertain terms that he had been foolish to rely on the King of Syria rather than God to rescue him from a powerful opposing army. The king did not appreciate such feedback. "Then Asa was angry with the seer, and put him in prison, for he was enraged at him because of this" (2 Chronicles 16:10).

Everyone will experience criticism at one point. We are not perfect nor are our choices always pleasing to everybody. Therefore, one of the best things we can do for our professional and emotional well-being is to get comfortable with criticism. Now, I admit that criticism often hurts because at its core, it is an *evaluation of our judgment.* Someone has decided that we have said or done something wrong. This can often provoke hurt feelings and anger even when it is done constructively. In such a moment, depending on our personal history or our confidence level, we may feel rejected, disconnected, and unsupported by our critic.

When you find yourself becoming angry when your behavior or choices are evaluated or criticized, try these strategies:

- Consider the source and ask God to help you discern the person's true motivation. Ask yourself: *Has this person demonstrated care or support of me in the past? What does he have to gain personally if I make this change?*

- Always listen with an intent to really understand and benefit from the input. Without it, you might not improve your skills or habits to become more productive or successful. Really engage your critic. Ask him to cite specific instances of the problematic behavior. Repeat his criticism without exaggeration or hostility: "So, what you are saying, Bob, is that the current process is hindering productivity." If you're feeling resistant to the input, ask yourself if your ego or insecurity is working overtime and sabotaging your development. Be honest with yourself regarding any feelings of inadequacy the criticism has aroused.

- Pray for your critics when you feel the criticism is unwarranted. Call their names out in earnest intercession, asking God to change them—not just so life can be better for you, but that they may walk in the fullness of His love and favor.

- Even if the criticism is unwarranted, remain calm and pleasant. Demonstrate that you are open to feedback.

Faith Declaration

"I don't mind criticism. If it is untrue, I disregard it; if unfair, I keep from irritation; if it is ignorant, I smile; if it is justified, it is not criticism, I learn from it" (author unknown).

Day 22

Disrespected

*"Let every man be respected as an
individual and no man idolized."*
ALBERT EINSTEIN

"R-E-S-P-E-C-T. Find out what it means to *me!*"
These lyrics from Aretha Franklin's smash hit song
remind us that respect is often defined at the individual
level. When some people feel disrespected, they are quick
to show their wrath.

Consider the story of Sarah, the wife of Abraham
the Jewish patriarch (Genesis 16). She was desperate for
a child and weary of waiting for God to fulfill His promise to give them one. Therefore, she insisted that her husband sleep with Hagar, her Egyptian maid. When Hagar
knew she was pregnant, she began to treat Sarah with disrespect (verse 4). Big mistake! No way was Sarah going to
tolerate it. She treated Hagar so harshly that she finally
ran away (verse 6). God intervened and directed Hagar
to return home and submit to Sarah.

We all want to be respected. In *Love and Respect*, the
groundbreaking book that prioritized the needs of men
and women in marriage, Emerson Eggerichs explains

that respect is a man's greatest need. My late spiritual mentor often cautioned us wives-in-training, "A man will leave a woman he loves for one who respects him."

Disrespect is rampant in our society. Doctors disrespect patients when they keep them waiting for an eternity—as if only their time matters. Retailers disrespect customers when they do not give their complaints priority or when their clerks display a negative, uncaring attitude. Children disrespect their parents when they rebel against their boundaries. Bosses disrespect employees when they reprimand them publicly. In many situations, the victim may not confront the disrespect, but the unresolved anger it engenders will eventually manifest itself in a negative way.

Feeling disrespected is one of the emotions most commonly tied to violent responses in adolescents and adults. When we are denied respect, we easily become enraged and can quickly lose control of our responsible reactions.

One day, while waiting at a stoplight, I accidently rolled my car into the back of a brand-new BMW (no, I wasn't on a cell phone!). It was only a slight nudge. I could see there was no damage to the vehicle, so I thought nothing more of it. When the light changed, I saw the driver pull over to the right while I kept straight on my merry way. A few blocks later, the driver whipped around me and beckoned me to pull over. He was dressed like the stereotypical gang member in the movies. He was clearly upset. I was terrified.

"Why didn't you stop!" he yelled. "You don't disrespect me like that!"

"Oh, sir. I'm so sorry, sir," I said, deliberately over-doing the "sir" to demonstrate my clear intent to respect him. He checked out his bumper and came back to my side of the car.

"I could see there was no damage," I continued. "I guess I'm just scattered right now because I'm on my way to the hospital to see about my mother. I'm so sorry, sir."

I actually pretended to be on the verge of tears to appeal to any modicum of mercy he might have under-neath his tough exterior.

"Well, next time pay more attention to what you're doing," he said, still in a gruff manner.

"Oh, I will, sir. I promise. Thank you so much."

Boy, was I relieved as he walked back to his car! Deal-ing with those who disrespect us can be unnerving, diffi-cult, and even downright impossible when we try to do it in our own strength. It requires the fruit that only the Holy Spirit produces in us, including love, joy, peace, longsuffering, and self-control. Here is what you must do when disrespected:

- Make sure you have not done anything that caused the disrespect. Many morally compromis-ing parents fall into this trap and are bewildered when their kids feel it is okay to disregard their authority. Ask your child's forgiveness for past mistakes and commit to doing the right thing going forward.

- Accept the fact that we live in a fast-paced soci-ety where people are distracted, overworked, and often insensitive to common courtesies. Make some allowance for this reality when dealing with the public.

- When someone disrespects you, know that you will not earn his respect by getting angry with him. You might succeed in intimidating him, but you will not have his respect. Be careful to treat people with the same respect you expect from them.

- In ongoing relationships, confront the perpetrator and explain what behavior you need from him. If he shows resistance, calmly explain what the consequences may be if he doesn't cooperate. Be ready to act on your word.

Faith Declaration

I am not overly sensitive to the disrespectful attitudes and actions of others. I am led by the Spirit of God in knowing when and how to confront such behavior as well as implementing appropriate consequences.

Day 23

Betrayed

"Each betrayal begins with trust."
UNKNOWN

In May 2012, a judge sentenced Los Angeles detective Stephanie Lazarus to twenty-seven years in prison after a jury found her guilty of murdering her former lover's new wife. Lazarus had spent more than twenty years concealing the crime she committed following the betrayal she felt when her boyfriend chose the victim over her.

Betrayal is devastating because it destroys the foundation of every meaningful relationship—trust. It is common in everyday life. A spouse or significant other seeks the arms of another after pledging undying love to you. Siblings divulge information you told them in confidence. Coworkers smile in your face while trying to take your place. The list is endless. Rare is the person who can manage the primary emotion of feeling betrayed without advancing to the secondary emotion of anger. Most will desire or seek revenge.

I still have vivid memories of being betrayed many years ago by Suzy, one of my protégés. I had invested significant time mentoring her spiritually, socially, and professionally. I had used my influence to open doors to several career opportunities for her. Then, when I made the unwise decision to bring her into my own corporate environment, she wreaked havoc by sowing seeds of discord between me and my staff, fabricating stories that I accused fellow managers of incompetence, and being insubordinate in staff meetings. I was devastated. I wanted to understand her motives. Even after some discussion with her, I could only conclude that envy had gotten the best of her. When I cried out to the Lord for wisdom in handling the situation, I simply heard in my spirit, "Learn from the burn, but forgive to live."

Acts of betrayal—real or perceived—are as old as the Bible. Consider the story of King Saul. He became insanely jealous of David when the people literally sang David's praises for killing Goliath the giant. The insecure king, fearing David would take his throne, set out to kill him. David became one of the most wanted fugitives of all time.

To make matters worse, David and Saul's son Jonathan enjoyed a close bond that transcended family ties. Saul considered Jonathan's fierce loyalty to David an act of betrayal. On one occasion, he even attempted to kill Jonathan with his spear (1 Samuel 20:33).

Later in the saga, we read that Ahimelech the priest unwittingly supported David while he was on the run by giving him food, inquiring of God for him, and giving him Goliath's sword (1 Samuel 21–22). Doeg, Saul's chief herdsman, witnessed the whole thing and squealed on the priest. Saul was livid! How dare Ahimelech offer such support to his enemy. Saul ordered Doeg to kill Ahimelech and all the other priests (eighty-five in all), their families, and their animals. In fact, he had the entire city of Nob, the town of the priests, destroyed. This slaughter was based on Saul's *perception* of a betrayal and his retaliation. Of course, a person's perception is his reality; thus, it would have been futile for anyone to try to convince Saul that Ahimelech had not deliberately betrayed him.

Jesus understood betrayal. Judas, a member of His inner circle, betrayed Him for thirty pieces of silver and set Him up for crucifixion (Matthew 26:14-16). Surely, Jesus would have forgiven him for his treacherous act just as He did Peter for denying Him. Unfortunately, the remorseful Judas couldn't forgive himself, so he committed suicide. Don't think for a moment that your betrayer is having a picnic. He is most likely having remorseful thoughts as well.

When someone betrays us, we often become angry with ourselves for trusting that person in the first place. We question our ability to judge the character of others. Such self-punishing thoughts buy us nothing but inner turmoil and keep us stuck in the pain of the betrayal. There is a better way. The guidelines below will get you off the road of self-doubt and revenge and back onto the path of trust.

- Maintain a divine perspective. Jesus knew that Judas's betrayal figured into His destiny as humankind's sacrificial lamb. God must surely have a higher purpose in allowing you to experience a betrayal. Trust Him to reveal it to you. Trust Him even if He doesn't reveal the purpose for it.

- Don't blame yourself or look for ways to justify or excuse the betrayal, especially spousal betrayal. You did not make your spouse cheat. Some spouses cheat because they do not have the courage or the communication skills to express their disappointments, desires, or expectations. Some are too naïve to see it coming. Still others rely too much on their own strength to resist the temptation. People are ultimately responsible for their moral choices.

- Determine what you want to say to the offender. Practice expressing it in a calm, collected, and powerful manner. You don't want to dishonor God by losing it and resorting to profanity or violence. Be very clear about your disappointment and hurt.

- Cast down thoughts of revenge; that's God's job. "'Vengeance is Mine, I will repay,' says the Lord" (Hebrews 10:30). Know that even relating the incident to others can turn into an act of revenge or retaliation as you destroy the perpetrator's reputation or ruin her image in their eyes.

- Prayerfully determine whether you should *salvage* or *sever* the relationship. This is not a decision whether to forgive; forgiveness is mandatory. "And be kind to one another, tenderhearted, forgiving one another, even as God in Christ forgave you" (Ephesians 4:32). Consider that God just may want you to continue to enjoy other benefits of being in the betrayer's life. If you decide to salvage the relationship, be clear about what you want or expect the person to do to earn back your trust. This is not the time to be vague in your communication or to insist that the person should just know; some people really are clueless when it comes to relationships. Evaluate how willing the person is to do the work of changing; any resistance to counseling, classes, or accountability could be a red flag—and a prelude to a repeat occurrence.

- As difficult as it may be, today is a good time to commit to letting go of the past. There really is no need to keep rehearsing the incident or to manipulate the offender with constant guilt trips. "And when sins have been forgiven, there is no need to offer any more sacrifices" (Hebrews 10:18 NLT). If the person has genuinely repented, God is not requiring more sacrifices; neither should you.

- Going forward, pay attention to your God-given intuition. Trust your doubts, perceptions, or nagging feelings about another person's motives. Don't ignore or rationalize away the red flags. Be proactive in getting clarity about what's really going on. Don't worry about being labeled as insecure for asking questions.

- Resist the temptation to develop a general mistrust of people. Treat a betrayal as a stand-alone event. Don't paint the entire human race or an entire gender with the same broad brush. Not all men are dogs, not all women are gold diggers, not all church people are hypocrites. Keep setting—and expressing—clear boundaries and reasonable expectations.

Faith Declaration

I honor my heavenly Father as the Governor of every circumstance that comes into my life. His thoughts toward me are for good, to give me a future and a hope (Jeremiah 29:11).

Day 24

Offended

*For in many things we offend all. If any man
offend not in word, the same is a perfect man,
and able also to bridle the whole body.*

JAMES 3:2 KJV

It seems that every week there is a news story of somebody being offended by something a politician, a celebrity, a pastor, or other high-profile person said or did. It has become an American obsession.

Merriam-Webster defines *offend* as "to cause to feel vexation or resentment usually by violation of what is proper or fitting." Within this strict definition, I find that most of us have way too many things that vex us.

For example, I used to get offended when thin women complained about their weight in my presence. The truth was that my sensitivity stemmed from the fact that controlling my weight has been a lifelong battle. Therefore, I allowed such comments to bring forth feelings of inferiority—even though, in all modesty, I had several enviable accomplishments and privileges. One day I had an aha moment in which I realized that certain women who made such comments were indeed envious. By subtly highlighting an area where I struggled and they were successful, they were attempting to level the playing field. Seeking to understand their behavior, as well as my reaction, caused me to stop being offended and to start empathizing with their feelings of inferiority. I believe in some instances their actions may have been done subconsciously. I have long held that most people who offend us do not do so intentionally.

What about you? If you dislike some physical aspect of your being, have you also discounted your awesome intellect? Are you insecure about being short? What about your pleasing personality? Are you sensitive about not graduating from college? Most millionaires didn't either! Stop devaluing your contribution to the world because of one aspect of your life that you have chosen to remain sensitive about. Rather, why not begin a desensitizing campaign. Seek to understand the behavior of people who offend you.

Now, let me quickly caution that this is by no means a suggestion for you to keep quiet for the sake of peace about every offense. It would be unbiblical (see Matthew 18:15 and Luke 17:3) and emotionally unhealthy to send the anger underground. There are legitimate things that other people say or do that are indeed offensive. Here are some strategies for handling those instances:

- Define what general behaviors will qualify as offensive. For me, it will only be when someone attacks my core beliefs and values (such as movies or TV shows that denigrate biblical principles) or when they violate my rights (race or gender discrimination). Otherwise, I will respect everybody's right to have his own perspective on an issue.

- Confront undesirable behavior according to the pattern set by Jesus. "Moreover if your brother sins against you, go and tell him his fault between you and him alone. If he hears you, you have gained your brother" (Matthew 18:15). I use this model when confronting Christians and non-Christians.

- If someone makes a casual comment in a general setting, don't take it personally and assume it was directed at you. We cannot expect people to be aware of our personal history and all of our sensitivities. Use the incident as a learning experience. Also consider whether the comment is a reminder that you need to make a change.

- In an ongoing relationship (spouse, friend, boss), it is critical that you tell the person how his comments or actions affected you. It is unfair to fume, fret, go silent, or expect others to discern why you are upset. Simply say, "When you said (or did) X, I felt Y. What was your objective in saying (or doing) that? I need you to stop." Keep your tone cordial and nonaccusatory. In my book *Confronting Without Offending*, I give step-by-step guidance on how to conduct an effective confrontation with those who have offended us. Read it to empower yourself with this often dreaded but necessary tool of communication.[8]

- Don't let fear of the offender's reaction cause you to delay in confronting him about his hurtful words and behaviors. The longer the time from the offense to the confrontation, the more likely you are to make erroneous assumptions about the person's motives. An effective confrontation is done prayerfully, promptly, purposefully, personally, privately, and peacefully.[9]

- Ask God for the grace to forgive the offender. Remember that we *all* offend people (James 3:2).

Faith Declaration

Wisdom tells me when to overlook an offense (Proverbs 19:11) or when to confront it. Either way, God is glorified in my response.

Day 25

Put Down

Don't repay evil for evil. Don't retaliate with insults when people insult you. Instead, pay them back with a blessing. That is what God has called you to do, and he will bless you for it.

1 PETER 3:9 NLT

Young David went down to the battlefield to take food to his brothers who were enlisted in King Saul's army. They were in a battle against the Philistines. When he heard Goliath the Philistine giant making one of his intimidating tirades against the Israeli troops, he simply asked what the reward would be for the person who would kill him.

When Eliab, David's oldest brother, heard him speaking with the men, he burned with anger at him and asked, "Why have you come down here? And with whom did you leave those few sheep in the wilderness? I know how conceited you are and how wicked your heart is; you came down only to watch the battle" (1 Samuel 17:28 NIV).

What a put-down! But David's response was superb.

"Now what have I done?" said David. "Can't I even speak?" He then turned away to someone else and brought up the same matter, and the men answered him as before (17:29-30 NIV).

In other words, David ignored Eliab without saying he was doing so.

I confess that responding with grace to a put-down used to be a major challenge for me, a self-labeled "come-back queen." Until I really understood the sinfulness of retaliation, I would return a verbal jab with an even more potent one—laden with syrupy sarcasm—all in the name of Jesus. Having seen my now-deceased mother experience the perils of being passive, I decided when I was single that there would be consequences to anyone who put me down, especially in my marriage. Thank God for the Holy Spirit, good spiritual mentors, and a loving husband who hasn't put me to the test.

Speaking of marriage, this is one of the primary theaters where put-downs are played out. The frequency of put-downs between couples is a major predictor on how long a marriage will last, say psychologists Cliff Notarius of Catholic University and Howard Markman of the University of Denver.

When [they] studied newlyweds over the first decade of marriage, they found a very subtle but telling difference at the beginning of the relationships. Among couples who would ultimately stay together, 5 out of every 100 comments made about each other were put-downs. Among couples who would later split, 10 of every 100 comments were insults. That gap magnified over the following decade, until couples heading downhill were flinging five times as many cruel and invalidating comments at each other as happy couples. "Hostile putdowns act as cancerous cells that, if unchecked, erode the relationship over time," says Notarius…"In the end, relentless unremitting negativity takes control and the couple can't get through a week without major blowups."[10]

Whether dealing with your spouse, family, friends, or coworkers, try these tips when dealing with people who put you down:

- Evaluate if a comment is indeed a put-down versus a sensitive button you have because of your feelings of inferiority in a certain area. For example, if you are sensitive about your height or weight, you will likely deem any related comments as personal attacks or put-downs.

- Look beyond the put-down and listen for the people's pain, insecurity, envy, unhappiness, or other motivation. Their comments will give you insight into their issue. Know that emotionally healthy people do not put others down.

- Do not respond in kind to a put-down. Resist the momentary satisfaction of retaliation. "Do not let any unwholesome talk come out of your mouths, but only what is helpful for building others up according to their needs, that it may benefit those who listen" (Ephesians 4:29 NIV).

- Develop some stock responses to put-downs and practice saying them calmly. "Thank you for your input." "Um, I'll evaluate your comments to see if there is merit to them." "Please elaborate so I can fully grasp your point."

- View any put-down as simply another person's opinion—not a final word on your value. People who are made to feel inferior often get angry. First Lady Eleanor Roosevelt said, "No one can make you feel inferior without your consent."

- Let people know you feel put down. This is not an accusation that their motive was impure, but the basis of an effective confrontation designed to get the issue on the table. In a marriage, a loving confrontation is a must. Say to your spouse, "I'd like for that wonderful, encouraging, affirming person I first married to resurface. I know he/she is buried somewhere under the put-downs. What can I do to coax him/her out of there?" Of course, if the put-downs continue, then you will need to take a more serious stance with stated consequences. "When you put me down, I won't stay in the room to listen. If the put-downs continue, the kids and I will take off a few days to give you time to consider your behavior." Only make threats that you have the courage to implement or you won't be taken seriously.

Faith Declaration

I am an effective communicator with a firm grip on my self-worth. Therefore, I do not retaliate or capitulate (accept as a fact of life) when I respond to put-downs. Rather, I lovingly confront the perpetrator and ask for a change in behavior.

Overwhelmed

From the end of the earth I will cry to You,
When my heart is overwhelmed;
Lead me to the rock that is higher than I.
PSALM 61:2

In March 2012, my husband, Darnell, was diagnosed with a life-threatening condition. While he waited for the doctor to schedule surgery, his brother Mike unexpectedly passed away. This was the third sibling Darnell had lost within a sixteen-month period. The family gathered at the hospital to support each other in absorbing the news.

En route to the hospital morgue on that blue Monday morning, Darnell received a call from his key employee advising him that he'd accepted another job; he would be leaving at the end of the week. The timing couldn't have been worse. It meant that Darnell would have to work crazy hours the rest of the week to get up to speed on the employee's pending projects. Besides, he was already working overtime in preparation for a six-week medical leave starting the following week. There would be little time for grieving or supporting other family members—a big deal as he is the spiritual go-to person in his family.

Darnell entered the hospital on Friday, May 18, two days after Mike's funeral. The surgery went well and we rejoiced at the news. In the meantime, I was juggling a publishing deadline, doctors' appointments for my elderly mother, and my speaking schedule. Darnell was released the next day, and I prepared to be his nurse.

On Monday evening, I received an urgent call that my eighty-two-year-old mother had been rushed to the hospital. After checking her out thoroughly, they released her. I insisted that she stay at my house a couple of days so that I could observe her more closely. Now I had two patients to monitor. Although it was my joy to serve them both, it was a challenging undertaking.

On Wednesday, as I was leading Mom downstairs for breakfast, she collapsed. Although the paramedics came within minutes, she passed away en route to the hospital. Suddenly I found myself in the throes of planning her funeral and the endless tasks that must be done (from selecting a casket and clothes, coordinating out-of-town relatives and guests, organizing the repast, fielding endless calls of condolence) while still ensuring Darnell's comfort and care.

When I took him for his post-op follow-up visit the day before Mom's funeral, the doctor advised us that there was a possibility the surgery had not been as successful as reported and the condition may have become graver. He had to undergo another test. It would be two months later before we learned that there was no trace of the condition. Praise God!

At this point, I found myself fighting the irritability

and impatience that can come when you face one adversity after another. Lashing out can become easy if you allow yourself to get into the mode of thinking you are overwhelmed. I didn't succumb to it. By the grace of God, I maintained my peace in the midst of the trying circumstances. Here are the strategies I recommend:

- Make it a point to worship God throughout the day. Sing songs of praise. Exalt Him as the Governor of every circumstance that comes into your life. This puts problems in perspective—divine perspective.

- Stop everything and develop a plan. Ask God, *What should I do next?* Then make a prioritized to-do list of tasks that will move you forward.

- Make self-care a priority. Disable your phones and get some sleep. Also, get out and exercise (even if only for five or ten minutes). It's a great stress buster.

- Ask for help and delegate tasks to qualified folks. Listen, if they are not qualified, it will only add to your stress level. Fortunately, I have many talented friends who had experienced similar circumstances and knew exactly what to do. I'm eternally grateful for them. Ask all other concerned people to pray for you.

- Assess your role in overcommitting yourself. Prayerfully consider resigning or taking a leave of absence. You may find anger lurking at your door because you are frustrated with yourself for not having the courage to say no to various requests of your time and energy.

- Know that when you feel overwhelmed, it's because you erroneously believe that you must resolve all your problems *yourself*, in *your* strength, and using only *your* limited resources. However, when you develop the habit of casting all your care upon Him, anxiety and frustration must go. During trials, I like to read 2 Chronicles 20:1-30 and remind myself that the battle is not mine but the Lord's.

- Resist the temptation to repeatedly say that you are overwhelmed. Such words sabotage your peace and thwart your faith. Throughout my ordeal, I kept saying, "The grace of God is carrying me. The Spirit is giving me peace that passes my understanding." I'm still marveling at how God seemed to put His hand over my heart and shielded me from the grief of my mother's death. (I should note that she'd suffered from dementia for the previous ten years, and I had already grieved the loss of the mother that I knew. It is a joy to know that she is now in a better place.)

- Meditate on faith-building Scriptures. Here are a couple for starters:

"Do not sorrow, for the joy of the LORD is your strength" (Nehemiah 8:10b).

"Come to Me, all you who labor and are heavy laden, and I will give you rest. Take My yoke upon you and learn from Me, for I am gentle and lowly in heart, and you will find rest for your souls. For My yoke is easy and My burden is light" (Matthew 11:28-30).

Faith Declaration

I am casting all my cares on the Lord, for He cares for me. I am acknowledging Him in all my ways and He is directing my path.

Part 4

Deal with the Nonemotional Anger Triggers

Day 27

Physical Pain

"God whispers to us in our pleasures, speaks in our conscience, but shouts in our pains: it is His megaphone to rouse a deaf world."

C.S. LEWIS

Have you ever stubbed your toe, bit your tongue, poked yourself in the eye, or accidentally inflicted pain on yourself in other ways? Did you immediately exclaim, "Praise the Lord!" or some other godly sounding expression? Good chance you did not! Or maybe you suffer from a chronic pain condition like rheumatoid arthritis or sciatica. If so, do you find that the pain lessens your tolerance for the shortcomings, annoyances, or offenses of others?

According to anger therapist Steven Stosny, anger is a response not only to emotional pain but to physical pain. "That's because anger releases epinephrine which numbs pain and gives a rush of energy. That's how athletes play with broken bones and why wounded animals are so ferocious."[11] Robert Emery, professor of psychology at the University of Virginia, further explains, "Anger shuts out pain, physiologically and behaviorally. Think about wounded soldiers who fight on and on, only realizing that they have been shot after the battle is over. In laboratory experiments, animals will tolerate more pain (electric shock) if they are given the opportunity to attack another animal."[12]

This may sound confusing, but what we have is a vicious cycle: pain fueling anger and anger masking the pain—preventing healing and perpetuating the pain. Studies have found that individuals who have anger issues are less likely to heal as well as people who are better balanced emotionally and can handle their anger well. The correlation between emotional stress and slowness in the ability to heal is well documented. Recent studies show us that people with anger problems have more cortisol, which is a stress hormone, present in their system, and this may be why they don't heal as quickly.[13]

While mental health professionals may generally agree that we are hard-wired to respond to pain with anger, this does not mean that we should succumb to such worldly theories and excuse our ungodly behavior as "natural." What about *gentleness*, that fruit of the Spirit (Galatians 5:23) that causes us to respond kindly despite our physical or emotional pain. Shouldn't this be our goal? You bet! Here's how to get there:

- Practice self-awareness. Know that when you are experiencing pain, you are most susceptible to angry expressions. Be honest with yourself about what's fueling your motivation when you are tempted to deliver an angry response.

- Address the pain. Many of us will tolerate annoying pain for years without seeking a remedy. I have put up with a slightly torn rotator cuff for several years now and cannot lift weights or extend my left arm over my head for very long. Consequently, I find myself being annoyed with my water aerobics instructor when he directs the class to do what seems like a zillion arm lifts. Clearly my procrastination in this area has diminished my quality of life. Outpatient surgery would fix the problem, but having had seven surgeries in my lifetime and a busy schedule, I've chosen not to invest in the necessary downtime right now— especially since I experience pain only when I'm lifting something above my head.

- Try alternative approaches to pain management such as acupuncture and special massages.

- Get plenty of rest. Muscle tension from stress or a lack of rest will only increase your pain.

- Don't pass it along. Anger is often a way of passing our emotional and physical pain to others. But is it really fair or wise to make others pay for our plight? Despite Job's emotional and physical suffering, Scripture does not record an instance in which he responded in anger. His frustration and bewilderment were clear, but he never let anger prevail. As our population ages, many will suffer from various painful conditions. Determine now that you will make every effort, by the grace of God, to resist becoming a cranky old woman (or man).

- Join a pain support group and learn how others cope with pain. This will help to prevent you from turning your daily interactions into "ain't-it-awful" complaining sessions that will ultimately cause others to steer clear of you.

Faith Declaration

At least I can take comfort in this: "Despite the pain, I have not denied the words of the Holy One" (Job 6:10 NLT).

Day 28

The Food Factor

*"Go and celebrate with a feast of rich foods
and sweet drinks, and share gifts of food
with people who have nothing prepared.
This is a sacred day before our Lord."*

NEHEMIAH 8:10 NLT

Nehemiah's exhortation to the Israelites sounded like a license to eat to their heart's delight. Indeed it was, for this was a day of rejoicing as the returned exiles heard and understood the laws of God. Yes, like the Israelites, we can allow ourselves to consume rich foods and sweet drinks during special times of celebration, but if we make them a part of our daily regimen, look out. There could be anger ahead.

Research has long documented the link between food and mood. "Food is not just something that fills our stomach. It's very active biologically and chemically, and it affects us," says Jack Challem, author of *The Food-Mood Solution*. "Your body needs vitamins, protein and other nutrients to make the brain chemicals that help you think clearly, maintain a good mood and act in socially acceptable ways."[14]

Here is a list of foods and drinks you might consider limiting or avoiding as they have been linked to aggression:

Sugar. Have you ever yielded to the temptation to devour a couple of cupcakes, cookies, or other pastries only to find yourself feeling on edge within minutes? Such *simple* carbohydrates (those made with refined sugar and white flour versus *complex* carbohydrates such as fruits and vegetables) give you a quick emotional lift by activating your serotonin, the "feel good" chemical in the brain that regulates your mood.

I confess that I have used Oreo cookies as a quick refuge from many frustrating situations. Such treats spike your blood sugar level (great for a diabetic in distress with no insulin in sight); however, they cause it to dip in short order. This crash makes you cranky and prone to angry responses or aggression.

A better alternative is to reach for a piece of low-fat cheese, lean protein such as turkey, or a piece of fruit. The results won't be as immediate, but the consequences will be less drastic. We must heed the wisdom of King Solomon: "It's not smart to stuff yourself with sweets" (Proverbs 25:27 MSG). Too much sugar can cause you to make a dumb choice.

Wheat and milk. Some people have an allergic response to wheat and the casein (protein) in milk products. The result is often inflammation of the brain, which can cause hostility.

MSG (monosodium glutamate) and artificial sweeteners. Their ingredients can heighten reactions, including aggressive feelings.

Caffeine. While caffeine improves alertness in the short term, the crash that follows can make you irritable.

Alcohol. Alcohol weakens brain functions that normally restrain impulsive behaviors such as excessive aggression.[15]

Trans fat. This is a type of saturated fat (solid at room temperature) found primarily in processed foods and margarine. Trans fat is actually liquid oil (unsaturated fat) that has been turned into solid fat by a chemical process called hydrogenation. This fat extends the shelf life of cakes, cookies, fries, and other junk foods.

According to the Harvard School of Public Health, at least thirty thousand people a year in the USA die prematurely from coronary heart disease as a result of eating trans fats. Thus, since 2006 food manufacturers in the USA must list trans-fat content on food labels. In addition to wreaking havoc on our cardiovascular system, trans-fat consumption is associated with irritability and aggression. So say Beatrice Golomb, associate professor in the University of California, San Diego School of Medicine, and her colleagues. They recommend that we avoid eating trans fats or including them in foods provided in schools and prisons.[16]

Not only can certain foods affect our mood, but the lack of food in general can also have a detrimental effect on our emotions. Have you ever become irritable and suddenly realized it was because you were hungry? I hate dieting—especially when, in desperation for quick results, I make the unwise decision to pursue a high-protein, no-carbohydrate regimen. It makes me so cranky.

If you are a perpetual dieter, then you know the agony of the first few days of carbohydrate deprivation. Rather than losing weight, you are more prone to losing friends as your irritability threatens to override your patience.

According to researchers at Cambridge University, when the body starts to feel hungry, your serotonin levels dip, causing a whirlwind of uncontrollable emotions including anxiety, stress, and anger. The fluctuating serotonin makes us prone to aggression.[17]

In 1 Samuel 25, we read the story of Nabal, a drunken rich man, who refused to give David and his men food despite their kindness to him and his servants. Had it not been for the wisdom and generosity of Nabal's wife, Abigail, who packed up a feast just in the nick of time, David would have slaughtered Nabal's entire household. Could it be that David's hunger caused him to be so irate that he became irrational? A popular drug and alcohol recovery slogan (H.A.L.T) cautions against becoming too Hungry, Angry, Lonely, or Tired.

Although certain foods and extreme hunger can trigger anger, we can be proactive in avoiding this pitfall by eating several small meals throughout the day that consist of protein, vegetables, and whole grains. This will assure a steady blood-sugar level. Be sure to include a few of the following aggression fighting foods: almonds, peanuts, walnuts, sunflower seeds, soy, unprocessed turkey, lentils, carrots, oats, broccoli, and avocados. We would also be wise to keep high-protein snacks (energy bars, trail mix, nuts) in our car, purse, or other handy place so we always have healthy alternatives when away from home.

Nutritional supplements are also important in fighting aggression. In a study published in the journal *Aggressive Behavior*, researchers found that giving prisoners omega-3 and omega-6 fatty acids along with vitamins and minerals reduced aggression by more than a third—as measured by the number of violent incidents that occurred in the prison.[18] Such vitamin supplementation is surely a good bet for the general public. Just remember to practice self-awareness as it relates to your hunger, avoid aggression causing foods, and pray for the wisdom of God in all your food choices.

Faith Declaration

I'm honoring my body as the temple of the Holy Spirit; therefore, I primarily consume food and drinks that are healthy and that fuel me for my tasks.

Chemical Imbalances

You will keep in perfect peace
all who trust in you,
all whose thoughts are fixed on you!
Isaiah 26:3 nlt

One minute my relative and I were having a normal conversation about a family matter, and the next minute he turned on me with such extreme anger, I feared for my life. His nostrils flared and his eyes were glassy. I had witnessed a couple of his outbursts against other family members in the past but, as unnerving as that was, it did not prepare me for a direct assault. When he completed his tirade, he stormed out of the house. I could hear him banging my car with his fist.

Later that evening, he returned with one of our more sober-minded female relatives. He was very teary and extremely remorseful. I was convinced that he had a brain-chemical imbalance. What else could explain a person going from zero to one hundred emotionally and then back to zero so quickly? I should also mention that he was a drug abuser.

Brain-chemical imbalance and its link to rage and

violence is a controversial topic. Some people believe pharmaceutical companies overly promote this premise to maintain their multibillion-dollar, chemical-imbalance-drugs market. Some of their more popular medications currently include Lexapro, Valium, Zoloft, Prozac, Topamax, Wellbutrin-XL, Abilify, Risperdal, and Zyprexa, to name a few. There is no scientific proof that any of these *cures* an imbalance. One psychiatrist explained that the medications are needed initially to get a person to the point where he can think clearly enough to make the required behavioral changes.

Here are a few basics of this very complex topic as they relate to anger.

The brain is an organ, the center of our nervous system. It produces chemicals called neurotransmitters that carry messages from the central nervous system to other cells in the body. Due to stress, aging, genetics, unforgiveness, and a host of other factors, these chemicals can get out of balance and cause the brain to malfunction. The following four primary brain chemicals must stay in balance to assure mental well-being:

- *Serotonin* plays a major role in dictating your mood. Low levels have been associated with aggression as well as poor impulse control—a major contributor to violence. Symptoms of an imbalance include depression, mania, low energy, sleeplessness, and low tolerance for pain. In the previous chapter, I highlight foods that are friends and foes of serotonin levels.

- *GABA (gamma-aminobutyric acid)* helps the brain to regulate the body's internal rhythm and provides us with the ability to manage stress with a better mental focus. Proper GABA levels help us to avoid bipolar disorder and its accompanying mood swings. Anxiety, lack of focus, feeling panicky, nervous, and having a low tolerance for stress may indicate an imbalance here.

- *Norepinephrine* helps to regulate moods and sexual arousal. It is also an important chemical in our "fight or flight" response when we perceive a threat to our well-being. Lack of focus, concentration, and motivation are a few of the indications of an imbalance in this chemical.

- *Dopamine* controls the brain's reward and pleasure centers and helps regulate movement and emotional responses. An imbalance here causes a person to become more self-righteous, condemning, sensitive to criticism, angry, and controlling. In severe cases, the individual may get more paranoid, more grandiose, have delusions, and hear negative voices.[19] Additional symptoms include low sex drive, excessive sleep, inability to gain or lose weight, and many more.[20]

Some Christians believe that a chemical imbalance is the result of demonic oppression. Others take a less severe stance. Paul Meier, a renowned Christian psychiatrist, explains:

Most people can correct these four vital chemicals by forgiving, confessing faults one to another (James 5:16), and obeying the "one-another" concepts in scripture. But lest we become too simplistic, some people have medical conditions, like hypothyroidism, that leave them depressed no matter what they do spiritually until they take the right dose of thyroid medication to correct the chemical imbalance. About 50% of the American population has inherited a genetic predisposition toward depression, perfectionism, schizophrenia, or bipolar disorder. Some of these people can NEVER become totally normal unless they take lifelong corrective medications, which work great. So if you are in the group that has genetic problems that make you depressed, manic, psychotic, or ADHD, no matter what you do spiritually, take the right medications, just like you would take insulin if you were a diabetic.[21]

Settling the controversy of the validity of a chemical imbalance is beyond the scope of this chapter. My goal is to raise your awareness of the various factors that may be at the root of uncontrolled rage in your life.

If you suspect that you may have a chemical imbalance, don't self-diagnose. Find (by referral or research) a highly regarded Christian psychiatrist as soon as possible. Further, you may want to consider the relatively new science of orthomolecular medicine (http://orthomolecular.org) that aims to correct a chemical imbalance with amino acids, vitamins, and minerals that are naturally in the body. A naturopathic doctor can also recommend natural supplements.

A few general behavioral changes may be in order as well, such as limiting your intake of caffeine, getting regular massages to reduce your stress level, confronting offenses in a timely manner versus fretting and fuming, and casting down distressing imaginations that keep your mind in a negative mode.

Finally, know that God is a healer, and no disorder or imbalance is beyond His ability. "According to your faith let it be done to you" (Matthew 9:29 NIV).

Faith Declaration

"Ah, Lord GOD! Behold, You have made the heavens and the earth by Your great power and outstretched arm. There is nothing too hard for You" (Jeremiah 32:17).

Day 30
Environmental Triggers

Now may the Lord of peace himself give you
his peace at all times and in every situation.
2 Thessalonians 3:16 NLT

Sometimes our irritations or frustrations are not the result of our internal musings but of the specific conditions or occurrences in our environment. Let's look at a couple of areas that bear this out.

Extreme Heat. Recently, I made a quick trip to the hospital in Riverside, California, to visit a relative who had just survived a life-threatening emergency surgery. The temperature outside was 109 degrees! As I was leaving the hospital in a mad dash to get back to Los Angeles (sixty miles away) to accompany another relative to an important doctor's appointment, the warning light on my dashboard indicated that I was low on fuel.

Oh no, I thought. *I'll have to pump gas in this heat. Ugh!*

I finally found a gas station and prepared to brave the high temperature. To my dismay, the pump malfunctioned when I attempted to use my debit card. A message on the pump display advised me to "pay the cashier inside." *More time in the heat.* The cashier told me I needed to go back outside and replace the nozzle securely in the unit before he could process my card. *Even more time in the heat.* I was not a happy camper. Knowing that extreme heat is one of my "irritation triggers," I purchased only a half-tank of gas to avoid more exposure to the sweltering temperature.

Fortunately, I had prepared for the heat before leaving home by bringing along a large cup of ice in an insulated container and a couple bottles of water. I always try to remember King Solomon's warning: "The prudent see danger and take refuge, but the simple keep going and pay the penalty" (Proverbs 22:3 NIV). I knew I'd be in danger of some negative attitudes and responses if I didn't take proactive measures.

What about you? Does your temper tend to rise along with the temperature? Many researchers believe this happens because we may have trouble sleeping, get dehydrated, and are restricted in our daily activities by extreme heat. Further, our lack of control over the situation can make us even more irritated. Thus, planning is critical if you want to keep your peace in the heat. Here are a few strategies that have worked for me:

- Drink lots of cold water to replace the fluids lost from perspiring.

- Get a small battery-operated fan (handheld or other) to carry along with you if you are planning an outdoor activity such as a picnic.

- Make a facial mist by combining in a spray bottle some water and Sea Breeze antiseptic (or a dash of eucalyptus, lavender, or other essential oil). Spraying the back of your neck and your wrists with this concoction throughout the day will keep you refreshed.

- Thank God for your salvation and remember that hell is real (Revelation 20:15)—and really hot. Your temporary discomfort from the heat pales in comparison to its eternal flames.

Clutter. Clutter is another environment-based trigger that can frustrate you and steal your peace—even if you are not a neat freak. Take my walk-in closet, for example. Even though I'm diligent in conducting purge patrols, keeping it clear of clutter is a constant challenge. During times when my schedule seems to be controlling me rather than vice versa, it's not unusual for me to take a week to unpack from a trip. My suitcase remains on the floor of the closet, and I literally trip over it a few times before I decide to stop the insanity. I feel such a sense of accomplishment when I take the fifteen minutes to put everything away.

The visual distraction of clutter overloads our senses and robs us of our tranquillity. Further, it reminds us of our failure or inability (when the clutter doesn't belong to us) to control our environment. A cluttered surrounding is often an indication of a cluttered mind and indeed a cluttered life. Frustration and low productivity are the results.

I actually stopped writing this book to organize my workspace as I found myself in a vicious cycle of restacking reference books and reviewing duplicate information written on notes in different places. Also, I still have stacks of sympathy cards I want to read from my mother's recent death. I'm reluctant to put them out of sight lest I forget them. I also have excess copies of her obituary, but it seems disrespectful to her memory to toss them.

Today, however, I found an answer to my dilemma in an old familiar place: the Bible. The writer of Ecclesiastes says there is "a time to keep, and a time to throw away" (Ecclesiastes 3:6b). This passage speaks very clearly to me. Effective today, I'll be rewaging my war against clutter. I'll ask myself only one question whether I'm dealing with the stuff in my garage, the trunk of my car, the various rooms in my house, or my office: What is the practical or emotional *benefit* of keeping this? I'll make a little progress each week.

Today I started with a single drawer; it felt great to throw out all those old cosmetics. I decided that I'm going back to my old policy of dumping or donating something every time I buy a similar item (clothes, shoes, books). Wanna join me in my quest?

Faith Declaration

The Lord of peace himself is giving me His peace at all times and in every situation.

Epilogue
Let It Go

I hope the preceding chapters have helped you to learn how to cut anger off at the pass by taking a deeper look at your irritation, frustration, or fury and what they are really telling you. I pray that you will embrace the practical ways I have suggested for how to respond in a productive and peaceful manner when tempted to become angry. If you are now convinced that it's okay to be angry or to experience anger, but it's not okay to sin as a result, then I say, "Mission accomplished."

Remember that anger is a God-given emotion and can be a real asset when properly channeled. It can lead to constructive outcomes; it can be the impetus for fighting injustice, for consciousness-raising, for exposing toxic, fruitless relationships, and much more. It never has to be associated with the intemperance of violence in your life.

I encourage you to let go of any and all lingering anger. This is a simple directive, but not always an easy one to implement. It starts with a decision to forgive, a commitment to letting it go. As Charles Stanley has written:

Forgiveness is the act of setting someone free from an obligation to you that is a result of a wrong done against you. For example, a debt is forgiven when you free your debtor of his obligation to pay back what he owes you. Forgiveness, then, involves three elements: injury, a debt resulting from an injury, and a cancellation of the debt. All three elements are essential if forgiveness is to take place.[22]

I leave you with a quote from famed Austrian psychiatrist and Holocaust survivor, Viktor Frankl: "Between stimulus and response, there is a space. In that space is our power to choose our response. In our response lies our growth and our freedom."

I encourage you to continue to be an example to the world of a child of God who takes responsibility for your responses and who gives God complete reign in producing in you the necessary fruit of the Spirit to help you walk in emotional and relational freedom.

Notes

1. "Paul Jennings Hill," www.clarkprosecutor.org/html/death/US/hill873.htm.

2. "How can you deal with your physical symptoms of anger more effectively?" http://gwired.gwu.edu/counsel/index.gw/Site_ID/5176/Page_ID/14129/.

3. Deborah Smith Pegues, *30 Days to Taming Your Fears* (Eugene, OR: Harvest House Publishers, 2011), 193.

4. Ethan Kross et al., "Social Rejection Shares Somatosensory Representations with Physical Pain," published in *PNAS (Proceedings of the National Academy of Sciences)*, 2011, www.pnas.org/cgi/content/short/1102693108.

5. To see the complete lyrics to this song, go to www.a-z-music-lyrics.com/song/?lyrics=I%20Still%20Have%20Joy&artist=Dorothy%20Norwood.

6. Daniel K. Hall-Flavin, "What Does the Term 'Clinical Depression' Mean?" www.mayoclinic.com/health/clinical-depression/AN01057.

7. Isa N. Engleberg and Dianna R. Wynn, *Working in Groups: Communication Principles and Strategies* (Old Tappan, NJ: Pearson Education, 2006), 140-41.

8. Deborah Smith Pegues, *Confronting Without Offending* (Eugene, OR: Harvest House Publishers, 2011).

9. Ibid.

10. "Putdowns Destroy Marriages," *U.S. News and World Report*, 21 February 1994, 67, cited at http://bible.org/illustration/putdowns-destroy-marriages.

11. Patience Mason, "Love Without Violence: Helping Parents Build the Powerful Self, a Workshop with Steven Stosny," *CompassionPower*, http://compassionpower.com/reviews.php.

12. Robert E. Emery, "Pain, Anger, and Hurting Back," *Psychology Today*, 23 February 2009, www.psychologytoday.com/blog/divorced-children/200902/pain-anger-and-hurting-back.

13. Bridget Webber, "How Anger Affects Your Wellbeing," *How to Relax*, http://howtorelax.me/featured-articles/how-anger-affects-your-wellbe ing.

14. Cited in "Angry? It Might Be Something You Ate…," *The Menopause Gang*, www.themenopausegang.com/index.php/newsletters/40-spring -2012/113-angry-it-might-be-something-you-ate.

15. Ibid.

16. "Trans Fat May Make You Irritable, So Get Angry," *EmaxHealth*, www .emaxhealth.com/1275/trans-fat-may-make-you-irritable-so-get-angry.

17. "Effects of Acute Tryptophan Depletion on Prefrontal-Amygdala Connectivity While Viewing Facial Signals of Aggression," Luca Passamonti, *Biological Psychiatry* 71, no. 1 (January 2012): 36-43.

18. Kristie Leong, "Reducing Aggression with Diet," *Health Mad*, http://healthmad.com/health/reducing-aggression-with-diet/#ixzz22S0 KGNk9.

19. Paul Meier, "Brain Chemicals Linked to Physical and Emotional Health," www.meierclinics.com/xm_client/client_documents/Radio Handouts/Brain_Chemicals_Linked_to_Phy_Emot_Health.pdf.

20. Eric R. Braverman, "Dopamine Deficiency, Related Symptoms and Conditions," www.hands2health.com/Dopamine.pdf.

21. Meier, "Brain Chemicals Linked to Physical and Emotional Health."

22. Charles Stanley, *The Gift of Forgiveness* (Nashville, TN: Thomas Nelson Publishers, 1991), 16.

Appendix

Anti-Anger Scriptures

But the Holy Spirit produces this kind of fruit in our lives: love, joy, peace, patience, kindness, goodness, faithfulness, gentleness, and self-control. There is no law against these things!
Those who belong to Christ Jesus have nailed the passions and desires of their sinful nature to his cross and crucified them there. Since we are living by the Spirit, let us follow the Spirit's leading in every part of our lives.

GALATIANS 5:22-25 NLT

Be not hasty in thy spirit to be angry:
for anger resteth in the bosom of fools.

ECCLESIASTES 7:9 KJV

Cease from anger, and forsake wrath;
Do not fret—it only causes harm.

PSALM 37:8

A fool is quick-tempered,
but a wise person stays calm when insulted.

PROVERBS 12:16 NLT

The words of the reckless pierce like swords,
but the tongue of the wise brings healing.

PROVERBS 12:18 NIV

A wise man fears and departs from evil,
But a fool rages and is self-confident.

PROVERBS 14:16

A gentle answer turns away wrath,
but a harsh word stirs up anger.

PROVERBS 15:1 NIV

A hot-tempered person starts fights;
a cool-tempered person stops them.

PROVERBS 15:18 NLT

He who has knowledge spares his words,
And a man of understanding is of a calm spirit.

PROVERBS 17:27

It is honorable for a man to stop striving,
Since any fool can start a quarrel.

PROVERBS 20:3

Do not say, "I'll pay you back for this wrong!"
Wait for the LORD, and he will avenge you.

PROVERBS 20:22 NIV

Whoever has no rule over his own spirit
Is like a city broken down, without walls.

PROVERBS 25:28

Don't sin by letting anger control you.
Think about it overnight and remain silent.

PSALM 4:4 NLT

Fools give full vent to their rage,
but the wise bring calm in the end.

PROVERBS 29:11 NIV

An angry person stirs up conflict,
and a hot-tempered person commits many sins.

PROVERBS 29:22 NIV

For God is working in you, giving you the desire and the
power to do what pleases him.

PHILIPPIANS 2:13 NLT

About the Author

Deborah Smith Pegues is an international speaker, award-winning author, a Bible teacher, certified public accountant, and certified behavioral consultant specializing in understanding personality temperaments. Her books include the bestseller *30 Days to Taming Your Tongue* (over 650,000 copies sold), *30 Days to Taming Your Finances, Emergency Prayers,* and *Confronting Without Offending.* She and her husband, Darnell, have been married for over 34 years and live in California.

For speaking engagements, please contact her at:

The Pegues Group
P.O. Box 56382
Los Angeles, CA 90056
(323) 293-5861
Email: deborah@confrontingissues.com
www.confrontingissues.com

30 DAYS TO TAMING YOUR TONGUE
What You Say (and Don't Say) Will Improve Your Relationships

Certified behavioral consultant Deborah Pegues knows how easily a slip of the tongue can cause problems in personal and business relationships. This is why she wrote the popular *30 Days to Taming Your Tongue* (650,000 copies sold). Her 30-day devotional will help each reader not only tame their tongue but make it productive rather than destructive.

With humor and a bit of refreshing sass, Deborah devotes chapters to learning how to overcome the

- Retaliating Tongue
- Know-It-All Tongue
- Belittling Tongue
- Hasty Tongue
- Gossiping Tongue
- 25 More!

Short stories, anecdotes, soul-searching questions, and scripturally based personal affirmations combine to make each applicable and life changing.

A 6-session DVD series, complete with a leader's guide, is also available. Each biblically based, 30-minute session is suitable for individual or group study.

30 DAYS TO TAMING YOUR EMOTIONS
Discover the Calm, Confident, Caring You

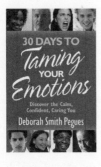

From Deborah Pegues comes an indispensable guide for overcoming the emotional barriers that rob men and women of life's fullness and derail their personal and professional relationships.

Pegues uses biblical and modern-day examples to help readers identify and overcome the obstacles that hold them back. Readers will discover emotion-taming strategies such as

- establishing boundaries

- extending grace, mercy, and respect to others

- conquering perfectionism

- accepting themselves and learning to laugh at themselves

- telling the truth and striving to do the right thing

30 Days to Taming Your Emotions provides Scripture-based principles, heart-searching personal challenges, and healing prayers and affirmations that point readers to a new sense of emotional freedom.

Compilation of *Supreme Confidence, 30 Days to a Great Attitude,* and *30 Days to Taming Your Stress.*

30 DAYS TO TAMING YOUR FEARS
Practical Help for a More Peaceful and Productive Life

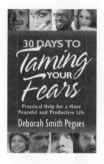

Deborah Smith Pegues, behavioral specialist and bestselling author, sheds light on rational and irrational fears and offers readers a path of hope and assurance.

With her trademark clarity and practical wisdom, Deborah addresses spiritual, relational, physical safety, financial, and emotional fears with godly principles and straightforward helps. Each step of the way, she gives readers power over fear by helping them understand:

- the foundation of their fears
- God's perspective on their specific anxiety, fear, or phobia
- how to respond to fear triggers with information, awareness, and confidence
- ways to embrace healthy fears and to resist unhealthy ones
- how neutralizing their fears maximizes their life

This will be an invaluable resource for anyone walking the minefield of constant apprehensions who is ready to exchange fear for the peace which passes all understanding.

30 DAYS TO TAMING YOUR FINANCES
What to Do (and Not Do) to Better Manage Your Money

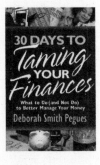

Deborah Smith Pegues offers friendly, doable money management strategies in this popularly written book.

Giving readers the benefit of her many years' experience as a public accountant and certified behavioral consultant, Deborah sheds light on the emotional and practical side of putting finances in order. The wealth of information readers will gather includes how to

- forget past financial mistakes and start fresh
- stop emotional spending and still be content
- fund future objectives with confidence

Each day's offering will inspire and motivate readers to savor the freedom that comes with organizing, valuing, and sharing their resources wisely.

30 DAYS TO TAMING YOUR STRESS

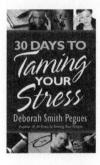

Deborah Smith Pegues leads readers to tame their stress and exchange it for peace in just one month's time.

With insight gleaned from her experience as a certified behavioral consultant, Deborah uncovers the surprising causes of stress and reveals simple, life-changing cures, such as

- extending grace, mercy, and respect to others
- telling the truth and striving to do the right thing
- accepting yourself and being able to laugh at yourself
- deleting stress-related words from your vocabulary
- reciting Scripture affirmations daily

This spiritual and practical offering will release readers from worry and will increase their sense of purpose, direction, contentment, and freedom.

30 DAYS TO A GREAT ATTITUDE
Strategies for a Better Outlook on Life

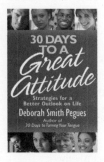

From Deborah Smith Pegues comes a powerful guide for conquering those bad attitudes that can derail your personal and professional relationships. Here's just a sampling of the attitudes Pegues tackles head-on:

- condescension
- control
- envy
- intolerance
- judgmentalism
- resentfulness
- self-centeredness
- sullenness
- victim mentality

30 Days to a Great Attitude uses biblical and modern-day examples to help readers recognize and overcome such counterproductive behaviors as expecting failure, putting down someone else's success, being indifferent to the needs of others, and criticizing the conduct or choices others make.

Scripture-based principles, heart-searching personal challenges, and healing prayers and affirmations will point readers toward the path to a new attitude.

To learn more about Harvest House books and
to read sample chapters, log on to our website:

www.harvesthousepublishers.com

HARVEST HOUSE PUBLISHERS
EUGENE, OREGON